Designing Data Structures in Java

A Software Engineering Approach

Albert A. Brouillette

DESIGNING DATA STRUCTURES IN JAVA

Copyright © 2012 Albert A. Brouillette
All rights reserved. No part of this book may be reproduced in any form or by any electronic or mechanical means including information storage and retrieval systems—except in the case of brief quotations embodied in critical articles or reviews—without permission in writing from the author.

Published by Microware Concepts

ISBN: 1481894366
ISBN-13: 978-1481894364

Dedication

This book is dedicated to those who,
with love, encouragement, and sacrifice,
made possible in the planning, writing, and production
of this book:

Nancy, my beloved wife,

My amazing children:
Michel, Amy, Nancy, Timothy, Thomas, Elise, Albert
and Michelle

And, above all, He Who made all things for His glory!

DESIGNING DATA STRUCTURES IN JAVA

Acknowledgments

Many thanks to the hundreds of my students
who have taught me over the years that
the love of learning
is the most important lesson
any teacher can ever teach.

And to the many teachers in my life,
in many settings,
who invested their time and
effort in me:
the most important lesson
any student can ever learn
is that not one of us is self-made,
and each is indebted
to the many who came alongside
on the way.

DESIGNING DATA STRUCTURES IN JAVA

TABLE OF CONTENTS

Introduction 11

Chapter 1: Programming is Problem Solving 13

Chapter 2: Representing Problems: Abstraction 23

Chapter 3: Data Structure Basics (Review) 31

Chapter 4: Arrays of Data 41

Chapter 5: Data Abstraction for Problem Solving 57

Chapter 6: Using Abstract Data Types 63

Chapter 7: Unordered and Ordered List ADTs 75

Chapter 8: Sorting 91

Chapter 9: Evaluating Algorithms 103

Chapter 10: Binary Search 109

Chapter 11: The Stack ADT 115

Chapter 12: The Queue ADT 125

Chapter 13: The Dynamic Linked List 137

Chapter 14: The Double-Ended List ADT 143

Chapter 15: The Dynamic Stack and Queue 165

Chapter 16: The Dynamic Ordered List 177

Chapter 17: Recursion *187*

Chapter 18: Doubly-Linked Lists *199*

Chapter 19: Binary Trees *209*

Chapter 20: The Binary Search Tree (BST) *215*

Chapter 21: Tree Traversal *231*

Chapter 22: Deletion *241*

Chapter 23: Heaps *255*

Chapter 24: Conclusion *271*

INDEX *274*

DESIGNING DATA STRUCTURES IN JAVA

> You've got to be very careful if you
> don't know where you're going,
> because you might not get there.
> – *Yogi Berra*

Introduction

Designing Data Structures in Java, A Software Engineering Aproach, was written as a textbook for computer science students enrolled in a typical, second-semester "Data Structures and Algorithms" (CS2) course using the Java language. The reader should be familiar with writing simple Java programs as encountered in a first-semester (CS1) Java course, including, at the very least: creating, compiling, debugging, and running complete programs; using simple data types, as well as *Strings* with their various methods; declaring and using objects containing data fields, constructors and methods; building *if-else* selection statements; and creating *while* and *for* loops. Those non-Java programmers with a background in programming, especially with those familiarity with other C-derived languages, will likely still benefit from the descriptions and illustrations, and will be able to follow along with most of the Java code presented.

The content here is certainly not intended as a beginning Java tutorial, nor as a Java language manual. It does not contain explanations of the Java library classes which implement some of the data structures discussed. Neither is the material arranged as a *Data Structures Reference Manual*.

DESIGNING DATA STRUCTURES IN JAVA

This book is intended as a step by step explanation and exploration of the how and why of using Data Structures in modern computer program development. Even though the Java language is used in the explanation and implementation of the various structures, the concepts are applicable to other languages the reader may encounter in the future. The topics included have been sequenced to build upon each other, always with the perspective of the beginning programming student in mind. There are discussions of software engineering concepts and goals, motivations for learning different data structures, practical applications, sections of ready-to-run Java code, and explanations of the way the code is written. The material emphasizes the 'big picture' view of good programming and software engineering practices, while also including real, working code that make the ideas concrete.

The goal of this text is to bring a beginning student, who has learned the fundamental concepts of the Java programming language, from the starting point of *novice programmer* to the next level of programming maturity. It is hoped that the journey will be both pleasant and fruitful.

A. Brouillette
December, 2012

> I'm like the everlasting optimist who fell off the skyscraper. As he passed the twentieth floor, the horrified spectators in the windows heard him shout, 'So far, so good!'
> – *Adlai Stevenson*

Chapter 1: Programming is Problem Solving

The Programmer's Task: *Solve the problem!*

Consider all the ways in which computers today benefit human beings. Personal computers allow users to play games, create documents, balance budgets with spreadsheets, solve complex math problems, analyze mountains of data, surf the Internet, and accomplish thousands of other tasks that could not otherwise be completed as efficiently or effectively. Computers in automobiles maximize fuel economy, minimize exhaust emissions, and monitor the condition of the engine and other systems. Kitchen appliances, such as microwave ovens, are controlled by embedded processors which respond to button presses, display the current settings, and control the operation of the appliance. In each of these examples, as well as innumerable other instances in everyday life, computers function productively because they are executing the instructions provided by their programs. Where did those programs come from? A person, or a team of people, wrote a computer program to solve a problem.

Computer programming is a creative endeavor in problem solving. Programming, at its most exciting, is the activity of everlasting optimists *(see the chapter quote!)*, who, facing the challenge of finding the as-yet-unknown solution to a problem, know that the answer is just around the corner, and that the defeat of their opponent, the *problem*, is only a matter of time... and some well-designed code!

The Software Development Process

Software development is one of the most *rewarding*, and yet, most *challenging* activities that human beings have invented. Software, amazingly, turns ideas into realities, turns tedious tasks into single button-clicks, and turns once-impossible problems into solved results. But herein lies the obstacle: due to the complexities inherent in making software "happen", *creating good-quality, properly-working software is a difficult task*. And, as the problem to be solved becomes more complex, the development of a software solution becomes *exponentially* more complex, due to the number of people and components involved in creating the solution.

As a result of this reality, the mid-1970's witnessed the development of a new engineering discipline. *Software Engineering* became an area of specialization devoted to the study and development of methodologies and processes for creating programs, *especially* those programs which are extremely large and complex. Learning from both successful and failed software projects over the years, the field of software engineering soon recognized four essential elements of problem solving which lead to effective and efficient software development.

Describing these steps in general terms, we can categorize them as:

- First, discover the details defining what problem is to be solved.
- Second, plan out the solution.
- Third, carry out the solution.
- Fourth, verify that the solution is correct.

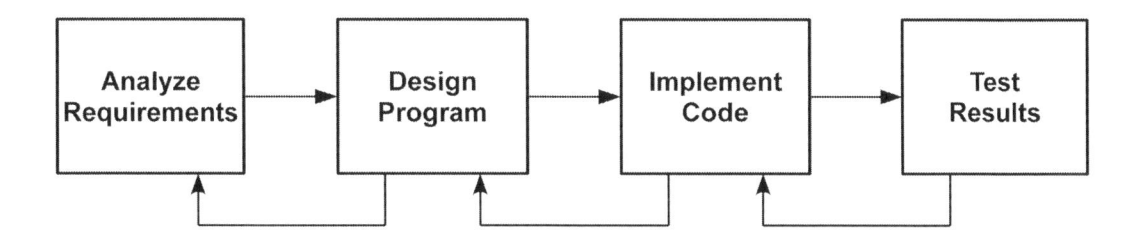

```
┌─────────────┐    ┌─────────┐    ┌───────────┐    ┌─────────┐
│  Analyze    │───▶│ Design  │───▶│ Implement │───▶│  Test   │
│Requirements │    │ Program │    │   Code    │    │ Results │
└─────────────┘    └─────────┘    └───────────┘    └─────────┘
       ▲                ▲               ▲
       └────────────────┴───────────────┘
```

Figure 1: *The Software Development Process*

This problem-solving process has much in common with any other engineering development situation. An architect creating a new home design, a mechanical engineer designing a suspension bridge, an automotive engineer improving a car's drive train, or an electrical engineer designing a new amplifier circuit, all utilize a similar problem-solving approach. In the context of software engineering, we refer to this process as the *Software Development Process*[a] (see Figure 1).

Restating the process using terminology specifically appropriate to the creation of computer programs, the steps are:
        1) Analyze the problem to be solved, defining what is required of the program
        2) Design the program data and algorithms which will create a solution
        3) Implement the solution by writing the program according to the design
        4) Test the program to ensure that it gives correct results

---

[a] The author has purposely compressed the wide variety of existing software development methodologies into a single representation here, in the interest of capturing the four essential elements of software development shown. Every credible development approach, such as *Waterfall*, *Spiral*, *Phased*, and even *Agile*, ends up incorporating these four elements into its processes in more or less recognizable ways, because these steps, regardless of the order or means in which they are fulfilled, are vitally necessary to the engineering process.

It is important to understand these four steps in some detail, as described below.

Requirements analysis- *What does it need to do?*

The most important step in the software development process is identifying the requirements for the project. The requirements must accurately address all the needs and intents of those whose problem is to be solved. The program requirements define both the purpose of the program, and also the criteria for measuring the developer's success. The final testing and validation of the software will be based entirely on whether it has fulfilled the list of requirements defined for the project. The program is, by definition, correct and complete *as specified* as long as it fulfills all of its requirements.

At a minimum, details for three particular requirements will need to be assessed for almost every computer program, answering the questions:

>What ***inputs*** will the program receive?
>What ***processing*** must the program perform?
>What ***outputs*** should the program produce?

The requirements must clearly specify all the intended capabilities which the program must possess, such as:

>What options must be available to the human user?
>How quickly must the program be able to perform important tasks?
>What types of reports will need to be generated?
>Which types of files will the program need to read?
>What information will the program need to store between runs?

The goal is for the list of requirements to be complete, and to describe unambiguously everything that the program must do.

The software requirements for a project describe exactly **what** the computer program is supposed to do, but, ideally, not specify the design issue of **how** it will accomplish it. The section below explains the justification for deferring design decisions until all the requirements have been specified.

Program design- *How will the requirements be met?*

The word *design* means, here, *to plan and to make necessary decisions about the structure of the program, its algorithms, and its data storage, based upon the specified program requirements.* A design determines precisely **how** the program will carry out the desired processing. Some of the common questions to be asked and answered during the design phase of the project include:

> How should the program functionality be broken up into program methods?
> What objects naturally appear in the problem?
> What will be the best format for storing any saved information?
> What should the user input screens look like to allow for efficient data entry?
> How should the menu options be arranged to maximize usability?
> How will we format the output so that it is most accessible to the user?
> Are there known algorithms for the needed processing?
> What data structures will maximize program efficiency?
> What reliability considerations are there when unexpected events occur?
> To what degree must the program be adaptable to new situations?

The overall complexity of the desired program will determine how many questions and issues must be answered in order to complete the design.

An acceptable design is directly dependent upon the set of requirements given. The two driving objectives of the *design phase* of a program are:

> 1) Every requirement must be incorporated into and satisfied by the design
> 2) The design must not include anything that is *not* specified as a requirement

To restate this in a more memorable manner: *The design must meet the requirements, the whole of the requirements, and nothing but the requirements.* Why is this important? The long history of the software development industry is filled with projects that failed to meet budget or schedule constraints because the software produced either failed to do all that it was required to do, or got side-tracked by added features that were not specified by the requirements. In large, real-world software projects, where multi-million dollar contracts may be involved, fully identifying the software requirements and creating a design which exactly meets those requirements are essential to any successful project.

Program implementation- *Converting the design into a working program*

The *implementation phase* of the program development process translates the design into compilable, runnable computer code. A good design makes this relatively simple, because all of the difficult conceptual decisions have already been made. Actions such as breaking the problem into manageable program pieces, figuring out the user interface, and determining the needed data elements have been completed, and a team of programmers can methodically transform the design into a working program with minimal effort.

The difficulties computer students encounter during the coding process are primarily traceable to starting their programming assignments here at this step, rather than at *requirements analysis* followed by *design*. Students often spend long hours attempting to code programs without first understanding the requirements and designing a coherent plan. This is a formula for wasting time, making very slow progress, and becoming frustrated.

Testing the program- *Does the program meet the requirements?*

The final measure of success for any computer program is this: *Does the program do what it needs it to do?* Ideally, the requirements correctly define the needed program; the design includes all of and only those specified requirements; and the code accurately reflects the design. Now, the *testing phase* of the process verifies that the program is correct.

Testers judge the merits of a program by determining whether it fulfills all the given software requirements. The program is subjected to a carefully planned sequence of test procedures which are intended to exercise all of the functionality contained in the requirements. Functional failures detected at this point will cause the program to be sent back to the programmers and designers for analysis, repair, and retesting.

It is easy to see how the quality of the prior work done will determine how quickly the testing process can be completed. For large projects with complex requirements, the testing process can represent a substantial percentage of the entire development cost of the project.

Measuring the Quality of a Program: FEMUR

A computer program is the product of human creative and intellectual effort directed toward a specific purpose. While it is impossible to measure the quality of programs using an absolute scale, assessing the *relative* quality is possible based on five common software characteristics. The degree to which a program exhibits each of these characteristics provides a means of deciding how well the program measures up to these quality standards.

The acronym **FEMUR** (which happens to be the name of the human upper thigh bone) provides an easy way to remember the five important quality characteristics of software:

> **1. Functionality:** How well does the program function, based on its intended purpose?
> **2. Efficiency:** How efficient is the program in its use of the CPU, memory, and other resources while running?
> **3. Maintainability:** How easy is it for a programmer to change the program source code when fixing bugs, adding features, or adapting to system changes?
> **4. Usability:** How intuitive, understandable, and enjoyable is it for the user to work with the program?
> **5. Reliability:** How trustworthy is the program in preventing errors and giving accurate results?

It is apparent that these characteristics cannot be measured using an absolute scale for every possible program. For example, the term *reliability* has different meanings and implications when discussing a word processor, a video game, a hospital patient monitoring device, or an aircraft weapons-targeting system. The definition of *usability* differs when evaluating a file compression program with a very simple objective, as compared to a professional-level drafting program which encourages the target users to obtain classroom training. Each program and characteristic must be evaluated based on how well the characteristic potentially could have been achieved under the existing circumstances.

Decoupling and Cohesion

In the world of engineering, and particularly software engineering, there are two qualities inherent in every excellent result produced. These characteristics are intuitive, once explained and recognized, but easily overlooked if not pursued through conscious effort. They affect all of the **FEMUR** software quality measures.

A *decoupled* system is one in which **the individual elements of the system are kept as independent of each other as possible**. This independence reduces the possibility of unintended consequences when one part of a complex system inadvertently affects another part of the system.

A system exhibiting *cohesion* is one where **each of the elements of the system are designed to contain only those parts which *belong together* in a useful sense, because they are related to each other functionally or logically**. This coherent grouping makes the system more consistent and easier to understand, use, and repair.

For software, achieving system decoupling and cohesion begins in the design phase, when the software requirements are being analyzed and categorized according to their functionality and relatedness. A design process where the conscious intent is developing well-defined and independent modules which *make logical sense* is on the path to an excellent design result. Ideally, a programmer or team will use an iterative design process of trying different groupings of functionality, and evaluating the groupings' independence and cohesiveness, and comparing different alternatives, until a quality design emerges.

However, the properties built into a design are not automatically well-enforced in the code, so the implementation process, too, must use the idea of ***encapsulation***, which means **programming the software elements using the data protection mechanisms of the language to enforce decoupling.** In Java, this means creating well-thought-out, independent classes which use the **private** and **public** keywords to control and limit access to data and methods within the class. Decoupling comes by making independent methods, or methods that are primarily dependent on other methods within the class, or methods that are dependent on other classes only through carefully designed interfaces. Cohesion results from planning the classes before implementing them, and thinking through how classes are identified, so that each class is comprised of only closely-related data and functionality.

Considering the **FEMUR** qualities in light of decoupling and cohesion, observe that:

Functionality of a program is improved when each part of the program works cooperatively, with the other parts, while maintaining its independence from negative outside forces.

Efficiency is encouraged when well-designed program modules prevent the duplication of code while isolating and optimizing the most time- and memory-critical software units.

Maintainability is improved when changes to any module have minimal chances of impacting other modules because of their independence. At the same time, cohesion means that related methods are all in the same class, reducing programmer searching for the correct location to make program changes.

Usability improves when the user interface exhibits a logical (cohesive) layout, and the task goals of the user are broken into understandable, independent (decoupled) activities.

Reliability results from building the software in well-defined, testable units which can be independently modified and improved as needed, without affecting other, already-working parts of the system.

Chapter Checklist

- ❏ Software development **is** problem solving.

- ❏ Computers are ubiquitous, solving countless everyday problems. Software programs allow computer hardware to operate in ways which are customized to their tasks.

- ❏ It is extremely difficult to produce large, complex, high-quality programs. Therefore, Software Engineering is the discipline which develops methodologies to improve the efficiency of software development methodologies.

- ❏ Solving programming problems involves four distinct steps: Analyze Requirements, Design Program, Implement Code, Test Results.

- ❏ Requirements Analysis is the process which defines what the software should do, without specifying design details.

- ❏ Program Design plans how the program will accomplish its tasks, ensuring that all the software requirements will be met. The design must meet the requirements, the whole of the requirements, and nothing but the requirements.

- ❏ Program Implementation transforms the program design into a program written in a programming language.

- ❏ Program Testing verifies that the program achieves all of its stated requirements.

- ❏ The quality of a program can be evaluated qualitatively using the five quality measures implied by the acronym FEMUR- Functionality, Efficiency, Maintainabilty, Usability, and Reliability.

- ❏ *Decoupling* and *cohesion* are qualities which improve software by encouraging maximum independence among logically and functionally coherent modules.

> **If you only have a hammer,
> you tend to see every problem as a nail.**
> *- Abraham Maslow*

Chapter 2: Representing Problems: Abstraction

Human beings are uniquely blessed with the ability to use abstraction in their problem solving. Abstraction makes it possible to create large, complex programs by redefining the problem in higher-level, simplified ways which are easier to manipulate and think about.

Defining *abstraction*

The word *abstract,* in conversation, is commonly used *(or misused)* to mean *vague, undefined, indefinite, difficult to understand,* or *intangible.* In the context of problem solving, **abstraction** has a specific meaning: **creating an effective, usable representation of a problem by preserving the necessary elements, while eliminating unnecessary details.** An abstract representation simplifies a problem by modeling it in a way that is easy to understand and easy to manipulate. Abstraction reduces complex elements by representing them at a higher conceptual level, and deferring the specification of details until later.

Problem representation is *everything*

One of the earliest abstractions a young math student encounters is the use of symbols to represent the concept of a *number*. The familiar Arabic numerals consisting of the digits 0 through 9 are used to represent numbers in the standard decimal system used throughout the world. In this system, a number such as '432' has the qualities of being both accurate and unambiguous. This means that anyone who is familiar with and correctly using the decimal system would always know that '432' means exactly four hundreds, three tens, and two ones.

The system is well-defined, and incredibly useful for representing mathematical operations. There exist simple, extensible algorithms for carrying out addition, subtraction, multiplication, and division of any decimal numbers of any length. For example, if someone has all the skills required to add any 3-digit number to any 2-digit number (such as 985 + 79), they will also be able to extend the addition algorithm indefinitely, and know how to add *any* two decimal numbers regardless of their lengths. The same is true for the other mathematical operations: once the minimal set of skills is learned for an operation, it can be used to solve longer problems which have never been encountered before.

Not all representations are equally useful

Consider another well-known but infrequently used numeric representation: the Roman numeral system. Given the mapping between the letter symbols and our decimal representation (Table 1), it is possible to unambiguously and accurately represent any whole decimal number as an equivalent sequence of Roman numerals. For example, '432' in decimal can be represented using the Roman numerals 'CCCCXXXII'. The addition problem mentioned earlier, 985 + 79, could be represented as:

```
    DCCCCLXXXV
+   LXXVIIII
   _____
```

REPRESENTING PROBLEMS: ABSTRACTION

It should be readily apparent that, unlike the decimal system, there is no simple and extensible algorithm for adding these two numbers when they are represented by Roman numerals. In fact, this number system is not effective for any mathematical operations, it cannot represent large numbers efficiently, the number of characters representing a number is not directly related to its actual value... the list of shortcomings is lengthy. It is no wonder that the system today is used exclusively for non-mathematical purposes, such as numbering clock faces, subdividing outlines, labeling the copyright year of movies, and identifying annual sporting events. Even though the Roman numeral system can represent numeric values accurately, the representation does not make it easy to do anything mathematically useful with the numbers.

Table 1: Roman Numerals

Symbol	Value
I	1
V	5
X	10
L	50
C	100
D	500
M	1,000

Another representation example - Chess

Figure 1: Physical Chess board

A physical chess board and pieces can be represented in a variety of abstract ways. Figure 2 shows the standard letter-and-number coordinates used to identify each of the sixty-four squares on the game board, such that the white king is located at square 'e1'. One way of encoding the location of the pieces would be through a simple mapping of each piece color, name, and position into a four-character code. The piece color will use *W* for *White*, and *B* for *Black*. The names of the pieces will be represented by

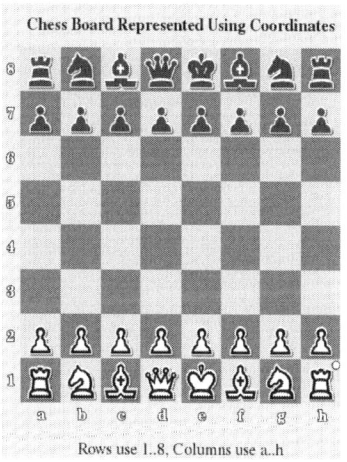

Figure 2: *Standard chess coordinate system*

the first letter of the name, with *K* for *King*, *Q* for *Queen*, *B* for *Bishop*, *R* for *Rook*, *P* for *Pawn*, and, to make it unique from the King, *N* for *Knight*. The position of each piece will be identified by its column letter and row digit.[b] This allows each piece to be unambiguously located with just four characters, apart from any other game context. For example, the entire configuration of the standard initial chess setup could be represented as:

```
WRa1; WNb1; WBc1; WQd1; WKe1; WBf1;
WNg1; WRh1; WPa2; WPb2; WPc2; WPd2;
WPe2; WPf2; WPg2; WPh2; BRa8; BNb8;
BBc8; BQd8; BKe8; BBf8; BNg8; BRh8;
BPa7; BPb7; BPc7; BPd7; BPe7; BPf7;
BPg7; BPh7;
```

It would be simple to store this representation as a set of strings in the computer, and the representation would be one that would be accurate and unambiguous– that is, any one who knows the encoding used could duplicate a physical board set up without errors due to inadequacy of the representation. However, a quick glance at the 'chess board' represented in this way reveals a problem: it is not easy to use when attempting to answer questions like, *"Is the White King in danger?"*, or *"Can the Black Bishop capture any White Pawns?"*. The difficulty arises from the fact that human beings are much better at perceiving the physical relationships among the chess pieces when there is a visual representation, such as appears in Figure 2. So, while the 'four-character' chess piece representation is usable for simply describing the board arrangement, it is unwieldy for attempting to play chess directly. Much like the use of Roman numerals when performing math calculations, this chess representation is not convenient for analyzing and solving chess problems.

---

[b] *This four-character representation is not the standard in chess notation, where additional context is used to present a sequence of game moves in more abbreviated form.*

Some data abstraction examples

Using abstraction, a 'thing', or, in programming terms, an object, is represented using only those properties which are relevant to the problem to be solved. In some cases, the choices for various representations of an object may be obvious. For example, if a problem calls for representing points in three-dimensional space, it makes sense to define an object which can represent a *point* 'thing'. Using programming terms, an object called *Point3d* might be declared, defined to contain three floating-point data elements representing the x-, y-, and z-coordinate values of a mathematical point. In this case, the *Point3d* contains essentially *all* of the defined characteristics of the thing it represents, the mathematical concept of a point.

As another example, consider the representation of an automobile. A car is a complex assembly of hundreds of individual parts and many different characteristics and options available. Representing *everything* about a car would be a daunting task. However, the data necessary for abstractly modeling a car will depend upon the required use of the model– that is, the problem to be solved. Suppose that a state department of motor vehicles (DMV) needs to store a list of the vehicles registered in the state. An object such as the following, defined below in Java code, might be sufficient:

```
class car{
        String make;
        String model;
        int year;
        String VIN;
        float mileage;
        double taxableValue;
        String licensePlate;
        }
```

Only the automobile features which are significant to the hypothetical problem have been represented. Although such additional features as the engine displacement, the sound system included, or the upholstery color are features of the real automobile, they are insignificant details within the context of the DMV need to store only the information it considers important. Including additional details would only complicate the registration listing, and would not contribute useful information to the task at hand.

In a different context, such as storing data for an auto sales advertisement, the engine, stereo, and upholstery might become significant features of the car to be included in the object. Alternatively, an automotive engineer designing the braking system for a vehicle would have little use for the fields included above, but instead might need to store the vehicle weight, horsepower, tire diameter, suspension characteristics, and other physical features which relate to the actual physics of the braking process. ***The best data abstractions contain only the elements which are needed for the problem solution being designed.***

REPRESENTING PROBLEMS: ABSTRACTION

Chapter Checklist

- ❑ Abstraction is a conceptual tool used to make problems easier to understand.

- ❑ An abstraction of a problem is a representation which attempts to preserve only the elements which are necessary to the problem solution, and eliminates extraneous information which is not essential to the task being performed.

- ❑ There are usually many ways to represent a problem, but some of those representations may be much more useful and effective in a given situation.

- ❑ Different problems require different representations, depending on the type of processing which must be performed, and the objectives to be achieved.

- ❑ The best data abstractions contain only the elements which are needed for the problem solution being designed.

DESIGNING DATA STRUCTURES IN JAVA

> If I had eight hours to chop down a tree,
> I'd spend six sharpening my axe.
> - Abraham Lincoln

Chapter 3: Data Structure Basics (Review)

Useful programs almost always have to store some kind of information as they are executing. Java programming students will already be familiar with the use of variables and objects for information storage. The intent here is to simply review the major data types and associated concepts in Java.

What is a 'Data Structure', anyway?

In a broad sense, a *data structure* is **any means of storing one or more pieces of information in a well-defined, organized fashion, so that a computer program can read from, write to, or perform operations on the information.** By this definition, a single variable can be considered a very simple data structure, an object is a data structure, and any way of grouping collections of variables or objects in an accessible manner would all be data structures. A shorter working definition is simply, **a collection of usable information**. Data structures are distinguished from one another by the manner used to access their data and their behavior in managing that data. The problem being solved determines which data structures will be most appropriate and useful in finding a solution.

The Native Java Data Types

A 'native type' or 'primitive type' variable is defined here as **a named memory location which can store one piece of data.** Simple Java variables are declared in this way (with optional comments shown in italics):

```
int counter;     //Counts loop iterations

double taxRate;  //Tax percentage to apply
```

Declaring a variable assigns it a name and also a *data type,* which defines what kind of information the variable can hold. Above, *counter* is a memory slot that can hold an integer value, and *taxRate* is the name of a place to store a decimal number.

Java provides several *primitive data types.* The most commonly used data types available to Java programmers are summarized here:

> **int**: Range: +/- 2 billion (approximately), stored in 32-bits. This is the most commonly used integer (whole number) data type, as its range is more than adequate for most problems.
>
> **double**: Range: +/- 1.7×10^{308} (approximately), stored in 64-bits. The *double* is the typical choice for floating point (decimal) values because of its accuracy. It can store fractions down to about 4.0×10^{-324}.
>
> **boolean**: Range: two possible values, **'true'** or **'false'**. It is used to store the results of boolean expressions.
>
> **char**: Range: character codes from 0 to 65,535, stored as a 16-bit Unicode character. A character is a single piece of information storing a single symbol of an alphabet, such as a letter, a digit, or a single punctuation symbol.

DATA STRUCTURE BASICS

Other, less frequently used Java primitive data types include the following:

byte- Range: -128 to 127, an 8-bit integer.

short- Range: -32,768 to 32,767, a 16-bit integer.

long- Range: +/- 9×10^{18} approximately, a 64-bit integer.

float- Range: +/- 3.4×10^{38}, approximately. The *float* can also represent fractions to about 10^{-45}. This data type is stored in 32-bits, and has less precision (fewer digits of accuracy) than the *double*.

Java Classes and Objects- Grouping Data and Methods

In the Java programming language, objects are used to create groups of data fields to represent one kind of 'thing' to the program. An object typically contains both data fields and methods (or functions) which operate on those fields. The combination of data and methods provide the functionality which makes the object useful to the program. An object is thought of as representing a *noun* in the problem description: a person, place or thing. Examples include: a person, an animal, an automobile, a book, a graphical screen element (such as a button or an entry field), or any kind of conceptual object which is significant to the problem to be solved.

The contents of an object are defined in a class declaration such as:

```
class Point3d {
        double x;
        double y;
        double z;
}
```

Here, an object to represent a three-dimensional point is declared to hold three *double* values, one for each of the *x*, *y*, and *z* coordinates of the point. Each time that a *Point3d* object is created, enough space is allocated in memory to hold these data fields. The following Java code is a simple example:

```
Point3d Point1 = new Point3d();
Point3d Point2;
//Set first point coordinates(5, 10, 3)
Point1.x = 5;
Point1.y = 10;
Point1.z = 3;
...
```

In this code, a *Point3d* object called *Point1* is created in memory using the **new** operator, and then its data fields are initialized. Another *Point3d* object reference called *Point2* is declared, but no object is created because **new** is not invoked. Instead, *Point2* is automatically set to the value **null**, which is a special name which Java uses to mean *"this object reference is not pointing to anything right now."*

Figure 3, below, gives a graphical representation of the object that was created, and the reference variable which refers to or points to it, and the reference which was set to **null**.

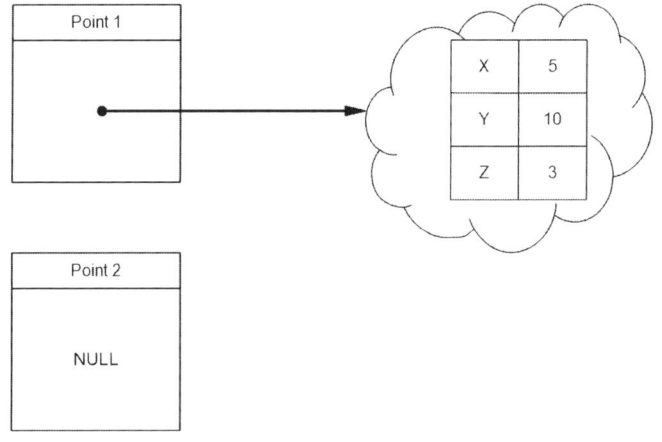

Figure 3: *Object References*

DATA STRUCTURE BASICS

Java Object References

In order to understand how Java objects work, it is important to understand the differences between *classes*, *objects*, and *object references*. These three terms are all related, but they have distinct meanings. Students often become confused trying to understand out how objects work because they have never really sorted out the precise meanings of these three different terms.

First, we can think of a *class* declaration as *the blueprint or template which defines what an object of that class will look like*. Thought of in this way, it is easy to grasp that a class definition does not actually allocate any memory space in the computer, but defines all that an object will contain when it is actually created.

An *object* is an instance of a class, that is, an actual, created data grouping built according to its class template. Objects are the *instantiations* of the 'thing' described by the class definition. Before it is used, an object must be created by using the **new** operator in an assignment statement like:

```
startPoint = new Point3d();
```

When an object is created using the **new** operator, memory space for that object is allocated on the system 'heap' (a section of computer memory set aside for this purpose). Any number of instances (objects) of a class can be created by using the **new** operator.

Finally, an *object reference* variable is a location in memory. The reference can either contain the 'empty' value **null**, or it can contain an address telling where an object has been allocated in memory. By using the reference variable, the data fields and methods of an object can be accessed.

A common error when assigning into object references

New Java programmers sometimes obtain results they did not expect from their programs when they assign the contents of one object reference variable into another object reference variable. Consider the following code segment, and the question which follows:

```
Point3d Point1 = new Point3d();
Point3d Point2;
//Initialize first to be at (3, 6, 9)
Point1.x = 3;
Point1.y = 6;
Point1.z = 9;
// Assign Point1 into Point2 (?)
Point2 = Point1;
//Set second (5, 10, 3)
Point2.x = 5;
Point2.y = 10;
Point2.z = 3;
System.out.println(Point1.x);
System.out.println(Point1.y);
System.out.println(Point1.z);
...
```

The question: What values will be printed out for *Point1.x, Point1.y,* and *Point1.z*?

The answer is: 5, 10, and 3.

But wait! Those are the values that were assigned to *Point2*... how did they get into *Point1*? In fact, only **one object was created** because **new** was only called one time to create a *Point3d* instance. The situation is shown in Figure 4. The key to understanding the result is realizing that this line:

```
Point2 = Point1;
```

-36-

does not create a new object, and does not copy any data between objects; instead, it just makes the variable *Point2* refer to the same object that variable *Point1* already references.

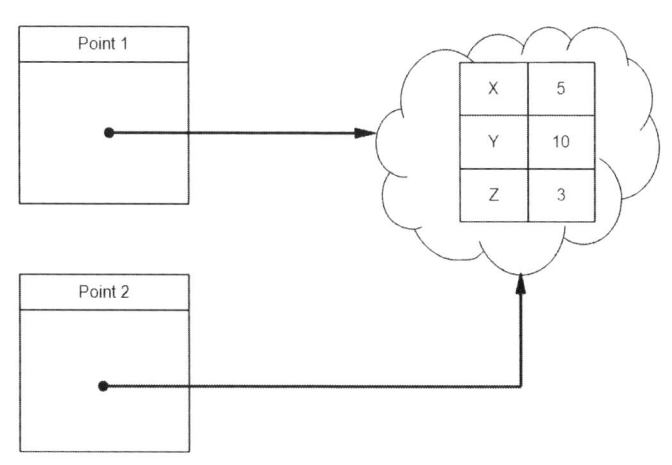

Figure 4: *Two References to the Same Object*

In reality, *Point1.x* refers to exactly the same memory location as *Point2.x*. The assignment statement placed the *reference* to *Point1* into the *Point2* variable. It may appear on the surface that this kind of reference assignment must always be an error, but it turns out there are very useful reasons to assign references in creating *linked lists*, a topic treated in later chapters.

Assuming that the intention is to create two distinct objects, and initialize them with unique values, the following code might be used:

DESIGNING DATA STRUCTURES IN JAVA

```
//Create both objects
Point3d Point1 = new Point3d();
Point3d Point2 = new Point3d();
//Initialize first to be at (5, 10, 3)
Point1.x = 5;
Point1.y = 10;
Point1.z = 3;
//Set second point to (3, 6, 9)
Point2.x = 3;
Point2.y = 6;
Point2.z = 9;
...
```

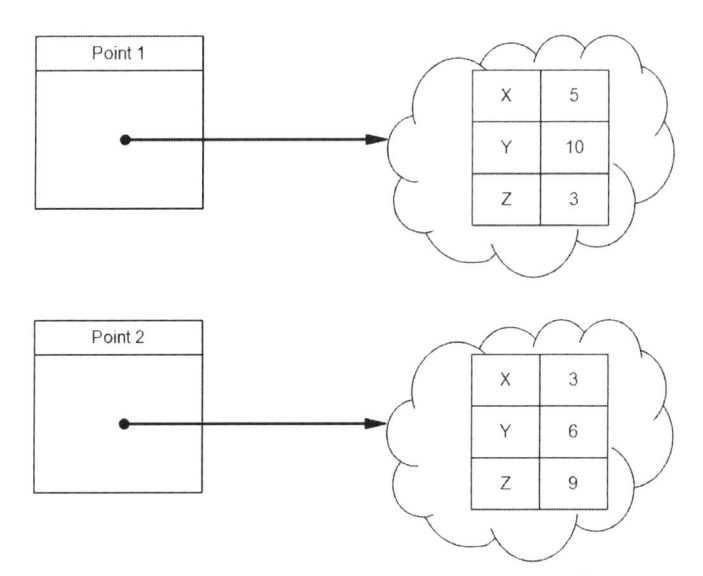

Figure 5: Two References to Two Distinct Objects

The result is the situation shown in Figure 5, where there are two distinct objects, each with its own allocated memory space. Reference variable *Point1* contains the reference to its object in memory, and variable *Point2* contains the reference to a different allocated object.

DATA STRUCTURE BASICS

The String data type

In computer languages, a string is defined as *a sequence of characters*, where each character represents a single letter, digit, punctuation mark, symbol, or space from some character set. Strings are useful for storing textual information. A *literal string* in Java is a sequence of characters surrounded by double-quote marks, such as:

```
"This is a string."
"Hello, world!"
"Please enter your name:"
```

The *String* data type in Java is implemented as an object. Unlike programmer-defined classes, the *String* may be allocated without the **new** function, for example:

```
String name = "Suzy";
```

would create a string reference variable called *name*, allocate space for the string, and initialize it to contain the characters in the word "Suzy".

Java provides nearly fifty useful built-in methods for the *String* type. A brief sampling of these follows, and a Java reference should be consulted for usage details:

int length()
       Returns the length of this string.
char charAt(int index)
       Returns the character at the specified index.
int compareTo(String anotherString)
       Compares two strings alphabetically.
int compareToIgnoreCase(String str)
       Compares two strings alphabetically, ignoring case differences.
boolean equals(String anotherString)
       Compares this String to another String, alphabetically.
String substring(int beginIndex, int endIndex)
       Returns a new string that is a substring of this string.

Chapter Checklist

- A *data structure* is any means of storing data such that a program can read, write, and operate on that data.

- *Native* or *primitive* Java data types are simple variables such as *int*, *double*, *boolean*, or *char* which can store a single piece of information.

- Java *classes* allow the programmer to construct the definitions for objects, combining data fields and related methods capable of processing data. Classes are abstractions of real-world 'things'. A class definition does not allocate space for any objects.

- An *object* is an instance of a class, and must be created by using the **new** operator to allocate space in memory for that object.

- An *object reference* variable can refer to an allocated object in memory, or can be set to the value **null**, meaning *pointing to nothing*. It is possible for multiple reference variables to refer to the same object in memory.

- In Java, a *String,* which is a sequence of characters, is implemented as a class. *Strings* have useful built-in functions, including: *length()*, *charAt()*, *compareTo()*, *compareToIgnoreCase()*, *equals()*, and *substring()*.

> What we hope ever to do with ease,
> we must learn first to do with diligence.
> – *Samuel Johnson*

Chapter 4: Arrays of Data

Java arrays are data structures which group a collection of like elements into a single entity. Arrays are often pictured as a series of numbered slots, each of which can store one value. *(See Figure 6, which represents an array of six integers.)* The data type of each array element is determined when the array is declared, and each array slot must be of the same data type[c]. Arrays are a kind of ADT, with an interface that emulates a physical column of storage boxes. Each box is sized to hold one item, and has its own identifying index number. The first box has an index of zero, and the other box indices count up from there.

Declaring Java array variables

Java arrays are constructed differently from the arrays available in many other programming languages. Arrays in Java are implemented as objects, and like all other objects, must be allocated on the stack before they can be used. Array variables may be declared in two different ways, which are similar except for the

---

[c] There are creative ways to get around this 'one data type per array' limitation, due to the fact that arrays can contain object references, as will be explained later.

placement of the square braces, '[]', in the declaration. Both lines in the code segment below are equivalent to each other:

```
int[] firstarray;
int secondarray[];
```

The inclusion of the '[]', in either line above, indicates that the line specifies an array reference variable. Here, *firstarray* and *secondarray* will hold `int`-typed elements, but arrays can be declared to hold any type of data, including arrays of user-created object types.

Because Java arrays are implemented as objects, all array variables are object reference variables. In the preceding 2-line code segment, *firstarray* and *secondarray* have been automatically initialized to null, meaning they do not currently refer to anything.

Creating array objects

In order to actually create the space for an array, as with all objects in Java, the **new** operator must be used, as shown in the following segment:

```
int[] firstarray;
int secondarray[];
firstarray = new int[100];
secondarray = new int[25];
```

Figure 6: *Array Containing 6 Integers, Illustrated as a Table*

In the example above, the **new** assignment into *firstarray* creates an array containing slots to hold 100 integer values, and *secondarray* is created with room for 25 integers. Java arrays always have starting indices of zero (0), and the last accessible slot has an index value one less than the number of slots available. Thus, the valid indexes for *firstarray* are from 0 to 99, and for *secondarray*, from 0 to 24.

It is common in Java to combine the declaration and initialization of an array into a single program line, so that the previous code segment might be shortened to the following:

```
int[] firstarray = new int[100];
int secondarray[] = new int[25];
```

In addition, there is a shorthand notation which allows the simultaneous allocation and initialization of an array, with automatic sizing, and *without* the use of the **new** operator. The following lines:

```
double[] xarray = {0,10,15,20,25,30,50};
double[] yarray = {275,750,1000,1100,1250};
```

create two arrays. The variable *xarray* is created to have seven elements, enough space for the seven initial values which are automatically placed into the array. Similarly, *yarray* is allocated with five slots, which are initialized to the five given values.

Using arrays

Similar to other programming languages, Java allows square brackets, **[** and **]**, to be used along with the array name to access the indexed slots of the array. As shown in the following code example:

```
for (i=0; i<100; i++) {
   firstarray[i] = 2*i;
}
```

the index for the array slot appears in brackets, after the array name. The **for** loop above counts from 0 to 99, and places the values 0, 2, 4,...196, 198, respectively, into the array slots. The index for a Java array must be a data type which holds an integer value, such as, a **byte**, **short**, **int**, or **long** type.

An array example

Following is a complete Java program using an array, with a number of different typical array operation examples. In this case, the array used is declared in a class called *ArrayUtils*, and several array-related methods are provided. Note that it is not necessary to build a class around an array, and that arrays are often declared and used in a program's **main** class.

The ArrayUtils class Java code

The *ArrayUtils* class is examined first. It contains the implementations for a number of useful array example methods. Explanations generally appear between the method declarations.

```
1  package arraydemo;
2
3  public class ArrayUtils {
4      //This array is public to allow direct
5      // access for illustrative purposes
6      public int[] array;
7
```

The data declaration section contains a single field, *array,* which is the **int** typed array upon which the methods will operate. Direct access to this field is provided by the **public** modifier. This is done in this example context to allow the user of the *ArrayUtils* class to use the standard **[]** brackets to index into the array. An example in the following chapter will show alternative ways of handling this *data hiding* issue in a more protective way. Likewise, all of the methods in this class are public as well.

```
 8  //Constructor creates the array
 9  public ArrayUtils(int size) {
10      array = new int[size];
11  }
12
```

The constructor *ArrayUtils* allocates space for the array, initializing it to the number of elements passed in the parameter *size*.

```
13  // Find largest value in array
14  public int maxVal(){
15     int index;
16     int max = array[0];   //set max to valid value!
17     // check each array value
18     for (index = 1; index <array.length; index++){
19         // update max if larger value is found
20         if (array[index] > max)
21             max = array[index];
22     }
23     return max;
24  }
25
```

The *maxVal()* method returns the largest value in the array. The int *max* is set initially to the first element in the array, and it will keep track of the largest value which has been seen so far in the array. In the **for** loop, *index* steps from the second to the last array slot, comparing each of them to the current value of *max*, and updating *max* if *array[i]* is greater. The built-in array attribute, *length* (accessed here as *array.length*), is used to determine how many items are in the array. The value of *max* is returned after the loop completes.

```
26  // Find smallest value in array
27  public int minVal(){
28     int index;
29     int min = array[0];   //set to valid value!
30     // check each array value
31     for (index = 1; index <array.length; index++){
32         // update min if smaller value is found
33         if (array[index] < min)
34             min = array[index];
35     }
36     return min;
37  }
38
```

The *minVal* method works essentially the same as *maxVal*, except that *min* is used to keep track of the smallest value found, and if the array slot is less than the current *min* value, *min* is updated to that smaller value.

```
39  // Find the sum of the array contents
40  public int summation() {
41     int index;
42     int sum = 0;  //keeps running total
43     // add each array slot to sum
44     for (index = 0; index <array.length; index++){
45         sum = sum + array[index];
46     }
47     return sum;
48  }
49
```

This method, *summation()*, initializes *sum* to 0 explicitly, a good programming habit, even though Java will set all numeric variables to 0 by default. It then steps through the entire array, keeping a running total by assigning *sum* as:
```
          sum = sum + array[index];
```
Finally, *sum* is returned at the conclusion of the loop.

ARRAYS OF DATA

```
50  // Calculate the average of the array contents
51  public double average() {
52      // length must be > 0
53      return summation() / array.length;
54  }
55
```

This method, *average()*, divides the sum of all the elements by the number of elements to return the average value of the array contents. This illustrates a method calling another method, in this case, *summation()*, to do some of its work.

```
56  // Multiply each element by multiplier
57  public void scale(int multiplier) {
58      int index;
59      // update each array slot
60      for (index = 0; index <array.length; index++){
61          array[index] = array[index] * multiplier;
62      }
63  }
64
```

Another illustrative technique occurs in *scale()*. The purpose of this method is to simply multiply each value in the array by the passed parameter *multiplier*. The method steps through the array, this time multiplying every array value by *multiplier*.

```
65  // Searches the array for value,
66  // returns the index of the first instance found.
67  // If value is not in the list, returns -1.
68  public int FindIndex(int value) {
69     int result = -1;   //default return
70     int index = 0;
71     boolean found = false;   //set true when match found
72     // search from index 0 through length,
73     //  as long as the value has not been found
74     while ((index < array.length) && (!found)) {
75         found = (value == array[index]);
76         if (!found)   //don't increment if value found
77             index++;
78     }
79     // if the value was found, return its index
80     if (found)
81         result = index;
82     return result;
83  }
84
```

FindIndex() illustrates a simple "linear" or "exhaustive" search method, stepping through the array and comparing each slot to the parameter *value*. Here, the means chosen for indicating that *value* is not in the array is to return a value of -1. The concept of *single entry- and exit- points* for methods will be discussed later. For now, simply note that the variable *result* is used to hold the value to be returned by the method at its conclusion, and there is only one **return** statement in any method, located as the last line in the method. The **boolean** *found* is set **true** if *value* is located.

A **while** loop controls the search, halting either when *index* increments past the end of the array, or when *found* becomes true. If *found* is true, *index* is the location where *value* is located in the array, and *result* is updated accordingly and returned.

ARRAYS OF DATA

```
85  // Moves the elements from slot start through length
86  // down to the next higher slot. Last value drops off.
87  public void moveItemsDown(int start) {
88    int index;
89    // Must count backwards or all slots = array[start]
90    // array.length-2 = index before the last slot
91    for (index = array.length-2; index >= start; index--){
92        array[index+1] = array[index];
93    }
94  }
95
```

Index	Values
0	10
1	3
2	25
3	8
4	19
5	16

Figure 7: *Array Before Calling* moveItemsDown(2)

Index	Values
0	10
1	3
2	25
3	25
4	8
5	19

Figure 8: *Array After Calling* moveItemsDown(2)

The method *moveItemsDown()*, and its complementary method *moveItemsUp()*, below, illustrate solutions to a typical kind of array problem: moving blocks of data within the array. In *moveItemsDown()*, the parameter *start* specifies the beginning of the block of data to be moved, and it is assumed that the block continues to the end of the array. The **for** loop counts down from *array.length - 2*, which is *one less than the last usable array index*, and finishes when it gets to *start*. Line 92 copies the value at *index* into the next higher-indexed slot, *index+1*, overwriting the previous value. Figure 7 shows an example array of six values prior to calling *moveItemsDown(2)*, which will move slots indexed 2 through 4 to the next higher index. Figure 8 shows the same array after *moveItemsDown(2)* has completed. The value 16 originally in slot 5 has been overwritten by the value 19 from slot 4. The value 25 in slot 2 can be replaced by a new value, since it has been copied to slot 3.

The code for *moveItemsUp()* appears below:

```
 96 // Moves the elements from slot start through length
 97 // up to the next lower indexed slot.
 98 public void moveItemsUp(int start) {
 99   int index;
100   // Count up, moving values up 1 slot.
101   // Last 2 slots will end up with same value
102   for (index = start; index < array.length-1; index++){
103       array[index] = array[index+1];
104   }
105 }
106
```

Index	Values
0	10
1	3
2	25
3	8
4	19
5	16

Figure 9: *Array Before Calling* moveItemsUp(1)

This method does the inverse of what *moveItemsDown()* does, at line 103 overwriting the value at slot *index* with the value found at *index+1* inside the **for** loop. The effect is to slide all of the value from the parameter *start* though *array.length-1* up to the next lower indexed slot. This is illustrated in Figure 9, showing an array before calling *moveItemsUp(1)*, and Figure 10, showing the results of the call. The value 3 at index 1 is overwritten by value 25 at slot 3, and so on, to the end of the array, where value 16 is copied up from slot 5 to slot 4, leaving both slots with the same value.

Index	Values
0	10
1	25
2	8
3	19
4	16
5	16

Figure 10: *Array After Calling* moveItemsUp(1)

```
107 // Print the contents of the array
108 public void display() {
109    int index;
110    System.out.println("Array:");
111    for (index = 0; index <array.length; index++){
112       System.out.println(index+"\t"+array[index]);
113    }
114 System.out.println("--------------");
115 }
116 }
```

The final method, *display()*, is a simple example of neatly printing the array contents. The *index* steps through the array and prints each of the slot values.

The main class of the example program

Now that the *ArrayUtils* class has been examined, the main class of a sample program is presented here, with explanations between the sections of code:

```
1 public class Main {
2
3 public static void main(String[] args) {
4    final int size = 7;
5    ArrayUtils data = new ArrayUtils(size);
6    int i;      //used as array index
7    int where;  //loaction where value found
8
```

These lines declare and allocate an *ArrayUtils* object having 7 array slots, **int** *i*, and **int** *where*, used later to hold the result of the *Find()* method.

```
 9     // fill the array
10     for (i=0; i<size;i++){
11         data.array[i] = 5*i;
12     }
```

The simple loop above initializes the array, filling slots 0..6 with values 0, 5, 10,...,25,30, respectively.

```
13     data.display();
```

The contents of the array are printed by the *display()* method call.

```
14
15     // get numeric results
16     System.out.println("Largest value : "+ data.maxVal());
17     System.out.println("Smallest value: "+ data.minVal());
18     System.out.println("Sum of values : "+
                                    data.summation());
19     System.out.println("Average value : "+
                                    data.average());
20     System.out.println();
```

Using the class method calls, the maximum and minimum values in the array are found and printed, as well as the sum of all the values in the array, and the average of all the values.

```
21     where = data.FindIndex(30);
22     if (where < 0 )
23         System.out.println("30 was not found");
24     else
25         System.out.println("30 is in slot #"+where);
26     System.out.println();
```

The *FindIndex()* method is demonstrated, showing how its return value can be used.

```
27      data.display();
28      data.moveItemsDown(3);
29      System.out.println("After moving down from slot
                                                    3...");
30      data.display();
31      System.out.println();
32      data.moveItemsUp(4);
33      System.out.println("After moving up from slot 4...");
34      data.display();
35
36      System.out.println();
37      System.out.println("Doubling array values...");
38      data.scale(2);
39      data.display();
40   }
41 }
```

The code above demonstrates calling the *moveItemsDown()*, *moveItemsUp()*, and *scale()* methods, then displaying the results using *display()*.

Example code output listing

As a final check on the reader's understanding, the actual output of the *main* class is given below.

```
run:
Array:
0            0
1            5
2            10
3            15
4            20
5            25
6            30
---------------
```

```
Largest value : 30
Smallest value: 0
Sum of values : 105
Average value : 15.0

30 is in slot #6

Array:
0         0
1         5
2         10
3         15
4         20
5         25
6         30
---------------
After moving down from slot 3...
Array:
0         0
1         5
2         10
3         15
4         15
5         20
6         25
---------------

After moving up from slot 4...
Array:
0         0
1         5
2         10
3         15
4         20
5         25
6         25
---------------
```

ARRAYS OF DATA

```
Doubling array values...
Array:
0              0
1              10
2              20
3              30
4              40
5              50
6              50
---------------
BUILD SUCCESSFUL (total time: 0 seconds)
```

This completes the discussion of the Java array structure. Future chapters will build upon the array material covered here. The reader is encouraged to solidify their understanding of this chapter before proceeding to the later chapters.

Chapter Checklist

❏ Arrays are indexed storage locations. They are capable of holding multiple values, each in a single storage slot identified by its index.

❏ Valid array indexes must be between 0 and (the total number of allocated elements)-1.

❏ Arrays in Java are implemented as objects, and their variables are references. They must be allocated in system memory, usually by using the **new** operator.

❏ Array slots are accessed using the array name and square brackets, like *myArray*[5].

❏ Arrays can be initialized with values using the following syntax:
```
double[] yarray = {275,750,1000,1100,1250};
```

❏ This chapter contains example algorithms, in Java code, for performing several fundamental array operations. The following operations should be understood to the level that the reader can easily write the Java code to implement them:
    1. Initializing the contents of an array using a **for** loop
    2. Finding the maximum or minimum values contained in an array
    3. Searching an array for a value
    4. Calculating the sum or average of the values in an array
    5. Performing some operation, like multiplication, on all array contents
    6. Moving a block of array values up or down in the array

> **The greatest difficulties lie where we are not looking for them.**
> *Goethe*

Chapter 5: Data Abstraction for Problem Solving

The concept of *abstraction* applies to the definitions of data types and data structures to help solve programming problems. An **Abstract Data Type** or **ADT** is **a data structure which specifies the kind of data that can be stored, the behavior of the data stored, and the operations that can be performed on the data, without defining any implementation (coding) details for how to build it.** This omission of the implementation details makes the ADT *abstract*. The ADT is a high-level description of a data storage mechanism. Usually, there are multiple ways to actually implement a given ADT in code.

The concept of an *interface*

An *interface*, generally, is a description of the manner in which two things interact with each other. For example, an owner's manual for an electronic device, such as an MP3 player, describes the *user interface* of the device. Included are a list of the capabilities of the device, a description of the functions of the display and buttons, a sequence of steps needed to navigate a file list, and so on. Ideally, there is a description of all the different ways that the user can interact with the device, and how the device should respond. This information contributes to the goal of using the device to its full potential.

However, the manual purposely omits volumes of detailed information, such as descriptions of the part numbers of the electronic components used in the device, the circuit diagrams, the algorithms used in playing music files, the system's internal clock speed, or any of a million other implementation details. These details are important to the device design engineers, and some of the information is needed for correctly assembling the player. But the inclusion of such details would be meaningless to the average user, and would be irrelevant to the objective of simply *using the device as intended*. The user is satisfied with simply having the *abstract* description of the device, without knowing its *implentation details*.

The ADT Interface

In a similar manner, the ***interface*** of an ADT is **a description of the ADT's available data fields and methods, along with any usage instructions a programmer needs in order to use the ADT effectively.** The interface tells what the ADT can do, how it behaves, and what methods should be called to make it function. The description of the algorithms, data storage, and actual code are purposely omitted from the interface as details which are not necessary to the use of the ADT.

Why *not* specify the ADT implementation details?

The advantage of keeping an ADT description abstract is that a programmer can write a program which relies upon the ADT without any need to know internal workings of the ADT. **As long as the ADT's interface does not change, any changes to its implementation have no effect on the code which uses the ADT.** This is an important idea which will be expanded in later chapters.

Data hiding, the key to good interface implementations

The best ADT interfaces define only those data fields and methods which are necessary for a programmer to use the ADT. This makes the interface as simple as possible, and maximizes the amount of control that the ADT implementer has in preventing the ADT user from inadvertent mistakes. This idea is also related to ***encapsulation***, the idea of building independent program elements (classes) which are protected from change or misuse through data hiding (see Chapter 1). The venerable "Murphy's Law" adage proclaims that "whatever **can** go wrong, **will** go wrong." One objective in designing an ADT interface is to minimize the number of possible things that **can** go wrong with the ADT.

The concept of *data hiding* improves the reliability of an ADT by giving the ADT user access to only the data and methods that are needed to implement the interface. By controlling what the user is able to do, many careless errors can be prevented. Some general guidelines apply when designing and implementing an interface:

- Data fields should generally be hidden from outside access. If the user does not need to know about the field, it should not be part of the interface at all.

- If a data field must be readable, create a "getter" accessor method which returns the current value of the data field, preventing it from being writeable.

- If a data field must be writeable, create a "setter" accessor method which takes the new value as a parameter, and when possible, error checks the value to ensure it will not cause an error, before allowing the field to be changed.

- Provide methods with the minimum number of parameters necessary to accomplish their intended purpose. Make method calls as simple and clear as possible, and name them appropriately with obvious names.

- Publish only those methods which are necessary to the functioning of the ADT, and hide all other methods. Make those published methods as harmless as possible, and include appropriate warnings to the user in the interface description wherever predictable errors can be generated by misusing a method.

The objective in these guidelines is to minimize the accessibility to the internal workings of the ADT in order to prevent outside users from naively making disastrous changes to data, or calling methods which have unintended effects.

ADTs and Java Classes

The development of ADTs as tools to assist in high-level problem solving occurred in the early 1970's. The concept pre-dates the development and widespread use of Object-Oriented Programming (OOP) languages by almost two decades. Therefore, it would be overly restrictive to simply equate ADTs with classes (or objects). ADTs were being implemented in non-OOP languages long before classes/objects were readily available.

In perspective, it is useful to think of classes, and the capabilities offered in OOP languages, as convenient mechanisms for coding ADTs. Java classes are the only practical means to implement ADTs in that language.

Java classes can enforce data and method hiding through the use of the **public** and **private** modifiers to specify the visibility of class data and methods. For simplicity, only these modifiers will be used throughout the sample code presented here. Methods and data of a class which are labeled **public** can be accessed without restriction by any other parts of the program using that class. Those class fields and methods having the **private** designation are visible only to the class in which they reside.

The following chapters illustrate the implementation of various ADTs in Java.

Chapter Checklist

- An Abstract Data Type (ADT) specifies the kind of data that can be stored, the behavior of the data stored, and the operations that can be performed on the data.

- An ADT does not specify how it should be implemented. This omission of the implementation details makes the ADT *abstract,* and allows it to be used without the any user knowledge of its internal workings.

- The *interface* of an ADT gives information about the data fields and method calls which are available to a programmer who wishes to use the ADT. In addition, the interface should include all necessary descriptive information about the behavior of the ADT and any method calling sequences which must be followed.

- The principle of *data hiding* seeks to limit the accessibility of the fields and methods of an ADT in order to minimize the error possibilities for a programmer using the ADT.

- ADTs are not exactly synonymous with classes. However, in OOP languages, classes are the standard mechanism used to implement ADTs.

- In Java, the primary data hiding capability lies in the use of the **public** and **private** modifier keywords to allow or restrict the use of data and methods defined within a class.

DESIGNING DATA STRUCTURES IN JAVA

> A thing continues to exist as long as is usual with things of that nature.
> – *California Civil Code,*
> *"Maxims of Jurisprudence"*

Chapter 6: Using Abstract Data Types

Abstract data types provide a powerful tool to the program designer, because ADTs allow the postponement of figuring out low-level programming details until the design is completed. The *IndexedList* ADT is provided as an example.

The Indexed List ADT Interface

The following describes the interface for the first ADT to be presented, the *IndexedList*. Here is a formal description of how it functions:

The integer version of the IndexedList provides an indexed data structure which allows data to be safely written to and read from an indexed location. Any attempts to reference an index outside of the existing maximum size of the list return a failure indication, but do not generate a system error. In addition to this standard array-like capability, elements can also be "inserted" into a slot, moving the other elements down to make room at that location, or "deleted" from a location, moving the lower elements up so that no gaps exist. There are also methods to access the maximum size of the list, and to find the location of a value in the list. The actual signatures of the interfaced methods are:

IndexedList(int maxLength, int errorValue) – *this constructor initializes the list to have a maximum size of maxLength+1 storage slots (legal index values from 0 to maxLength) and uses errorValue as the value returned from **Get()** if the provided index is outside of the range 0..maxLength.*

int Size() – *returns the initialized maxLength of the list, which is the largest index that can be accessed.*

boolean Set(int index, int value) – *assigns value into the slot located at index, overwriting the existing contents. Returns false only if the index is outside of the range 0..maxLength of the list, in which case the list remains unchanged.*

int Get(int index) – *returns the value of the list location at index. If index is outside the range 0..maxLength, the errorValue which was initialized in the **IndexedList** constructor is returned.*

boolean Insert(int index, int value) – *assigns value to the slot at index, after first moving the contents of all the slots from index to maxLength-1 up to the next higher-indexed slot number. The last value in the list, which was located at index maxLength, is lost. Returns false if index is outside the range 0..maxLength.*

boolean Delete(int index) – *deletes the existing value located at index in the List by moving the values from index+1 through maxLength*

int Find(int value) – *searches the existing list for value, and returns the index the first instance found (the lowest-indexed). If value is not in the list, Find returns -1, meaning 'not found'.*

This interface description explains the behavior of the Indexed List, but purposely does not define how this ADT is to be implemented. There are many possible ways that the list could be built using standard Java data types, but the interface does not specify a choice. Notice that the description of the *IndexedList*, although defined here to store **int** data elements, can easily be defined to hold any other kind of data elements by simply replacing the occurrences of **int** which refer to the stored data with the desired native Java data type or any user-defined class type.

Main program example code

Here is an example of a main program which uses the Indexed List ADT, without any knowledge of how the information is actually stored.

```
1
2
3  public class Main {
4
5  // A helper function to print an IndexedList
6  private static void printList(IndexedList list){
7      int index;
8      System.out.println("Indexed List Contents:");
9      for (index = 0; index <= list.Size(); index++){
10         System.out.println(index+"  "+list.Get(index));
11     }
12     System.out.println();
13 }
14
```

The *printList()* method (lines 6-14) accepts an *IndexedList* parameter, and uses its methods to loop through all the elements in the list, printing each index and value on its own output line. It is presented here to illustrate how the list data can be accessed, but its declaration could also be moved into the *IndexedList* class.

```
15 public static void main(String[] args) {
16    final int length = 4; //number of elements allowed
17    IndexedList data = new IndexedList(length,-99);
18    int index;       // indexes the list
19    int whereFound;  // location of found data
```

Variables are defined at the top of the *main* method (15-19). *length* is defined as a constant value *4* using the **final** designation, so that it cannot be changed. *data* is the name of the IndexedList being created to have *length* elements, and an error return value of *-99*, as described in the ADT interface. *index* is an **int** used as an index into the *data* list, and *whereFound* is used later to store the value returned by the *Find()* method.

```
20      for (index= 0; index<= length; index++){
21          data.Set(index, 2*index);
22      }
```

The **for** loop here (20-22) sets the values in the list so that each slot contains a value which is twice the value of its index.

```
23      // Display values
24      printList(data);
25      // Show result of bad index
26      System.out.println("Slot 50 contains "+
27                  data.Get(50));
28
```

This section displays the initialized list (24), then illustrates the result of calling *Get()* with an out-of-range index of *50* (26-27).

```
29      // Test Find
30      whereFound = data.Find(6);
31      if (whereFound >=0)
32          System.out.println("Value 6 found at slot "+
33                  whereFound);
34      else
35          System.out.println("Value 6 was not found.");
36
```

Next, the *Find()* method is tested (29-36), with a call to search for the value 6. The

USING ABSTRACT DATA TYPES

if condition determines if the search was successful, and prints the appropriate message.

```
37 // Test insert
38 System.out.println("Insert 27 at slot 3.");
39 data.Insert(3, 27);
40 printList(data);
41
42 // Test delete
43 System.out.println("Delete value at slot 2.");
44 data.Delete(2);
45 printList(data);
46  }
47 }
```

Finally, the *Insert()* method is used to place a new value of *27* at index *3* and the resulting list is printed (37-40), then the *Delete()* method removes the element at index *2*, and prints the results (42-45).

Example program output

An example of the output of this program is shown below. This listing should be compared with the source code above so that the output of each program section is completely understood.

```
run:
Indexed List Contents:
0   0
1   2
2   4
3   6
4   8

Slot 50 contains -99
Value 6 fount at slot 3
```

-67-

```
Insert 27 at slot 3.
Indexed List Contents:
0   0
1   2
2   4
3   27
4   6

Delete value at slot 2.
Indexed List Contents:
0   0
1   2
2   27
3   6
4   0

BUILD SUCCESSFUL (total time: 0 seconds)
```

Implementing the *IndexedList* class

This complete implementation of the *IndexedList* uses the already-familiar Java array type as its underlying storage mechanism. From a teaching and learning perspective, this choice provides some ideal opportunities. First, the array already has indexing, and is easy to apply to this application. Second, this provides a nice example of one class (the *IndexedList*) using another existing class (the array) while exposing a completely different interface from that of the underlying storage mechanism. The complete code listing follows, with explanations for each method interspersed.

```
1 package indexedlist;
2
3 public class IndexedList {
4    private int length;         // highest index value
5    private int errorReturn;    // value returned on error
6    private int[] storage;      // array to hold data
7
```

USING ABSTRACT DATA TYPES

The data storage for the *IndexedList* choice are all specified as **private**, and cannot be directly accessed outside of this class. The maximum array index is specified by *length*. To illustrate one approach to error handling and flexibility, *errorReturn* is set in the class constructor (below), and stored as the value to be returned whenever *Get()* is called with an invalid index. The list contents is stored in the **int** array *storage*.

```
 8  // Constructor initializes the list to have a maximum
 9  //   size of maxLength+1 storage slots
10  // Saves errorValue as the value returned on attempted
11  //   access outside the valid index range.
12  public IndexedList(int maxLength, int errorValue) {
13      length = maxLength;
14      errorReturn = errorValue;
15      storage = new int[length+1];  //allows 0..length
                                                indexes
16  }
17
```

The *IndexedList* constructor takes two parameters: *maxLength* is the highest index the user wants to use, and *errorValue* is the value to be saved in *errorReturn*, described above.

```
18  // Returns the initialized maxLength of the list,
19  //   which is the largest index that can be accessed.
20  public int Size() {
21      return length;
22      }
23
```

The *Size()* method simple returns the stored *length* value, effectively making that variable read-only for any outside user of the class.

```
24   // Assigns value into the slot located at index.
25   // Returns false if index is invalid
26   public boolean Set(int index, int value) {
27     boolean result = false;   //default return value
28     if ((index >=0) && (index <= length)) {
29        storage[index] = value;
30        result = true;
31     }
32     return result;
33   }
34
```

The *Set()* method allows for error-free access to the *IndexedList*. For illustration, it returns a **boolean** value, but it could have been made to match the *Get()* method's error return value as well. The default *result* is set to false, in case an invalid *index* was passed in. Line 28 performs a range check on *index*, and if it is valid, the array slot is updated with *value*, and *result* is set to **true**.

```
35   // Returns the value of the list location at index.
36   // Returns errorReturn if index is invalid
37   public int Get(int index) {
38     int result = errorReturn;   //default return value
39     if ((index >=0) && (index <= length)) {
40        result = storage[index];
41     }
42     return result;
43   }
44
```

The *Get()* method functions as the inverse of *Set()*, with the difference (for illustration) that it returns an **int** rather than a **boolean**. The logic is almost identical to *Set()*.

```
45  // Assigns value to the slot at index, after
46  //  first moving the contents of the slots below down.
47  // Returns false if index is invalid
48  public boolean Insert(int index, int value) {
49    boolean result = false;   //default return value
50    if ((index >=0) && (index <= length)) {
51       moveItemsDown(index);  // moves items down
52       storage[index] = value;
53       result = true;
54    }
55    return result;
56  }
57
```

Here, the *IndexedList* implements an additional capability over the standard array, through the *Insert()* method. Rather than overwriting the value at the specified *index*, as *Set()* does, *Insert()* first moves all the array contents from *index* to the end of the array down one slot to the next higher-numbered slot, using the same *moveItemsDown()* method encountered in Chapter 4's *ArrayUtil* class. Other than the data move, the logic is the same as *Set()*.

```
58  // Deletes the existing value located at index in
59  //  the List by moving the values from index+1
60  //  through maxLength up 1. False if index invalid.
61  public boolean Delete(int index) {
62    boolean result = false;   //default return value
63    if ((index >=0) && (index <= length)) {
64       moveItemsUp(index);   // moves items down
65       storage[length] = 0;  //zero out last value
66       result = true;
67    }
68    return result;
69  }
70
```

The *Delete()* method is analogous to the *Insert()* method. The logic is almost identical to *Insert()*, except that the data in the array from *index* to the end of the array is moved up to the next lower-indexed slot, overwriting the value at *index*. The *moveItemsUp* is the same as that in the *ArrayUtils* class.

```
71 // Searches the existing list for value,
72 // and returns the index the first instance found.
73 // If value is not in the list, returns -1.
74 public int Find(int value) {
75    int result = -1;   //default return
76    int index = 0;
77    boolean found = false;   //set true when match found
78    // search from index 0 through length,
79    //  as long as the value has not been found
80    while ((index <= length) && (!found)) {
81        found = (value == storage[index]);
82        if (!found)   //don't increment if value found
83            index++;
84    }
85    // if the value was found, return its index
86    if (found)
87        result = index;
88    return result;
89 }
90
```

The *Find()* method presented here is essentially the same as the *FindIndex()* code used in the *ArrayUtils* example.

```
 91  // Moves the elements from slot start through length
 92  // down to the next higher slot.
 93  private void moveItemsDown(int start) {
 94     int index;
 95     // Must count backwards or all slots = storage[start]
 96     for (index = length-1; index >= start; index--){
 97         storage[index+1] = storage[index];
 98     }
 99  }
100
101  // Moves the elements from slot start through length
102  // up to the next lower indexed slot.
103  private void moveItemsUp(int start) {
104     int index;
105     // Count up, moving values up 1 slot
106     for (index = start; index <= length -1; index++){
107         storage[index] = storage[index+1];
108     }
109  }
110  }
```

These two methods, *moveItemsUp()* and *moveItemsDown()* are identical to the same methods appearing in the *ArrayUtils* previously discussed. They are declared **private** here, so that they cannot be called from outside of the class, thus preventing erroneous use of these methods.

Chapter Checklist

- ❑ The *IndexedList* ADT described in this chapter is a simple example of constructing a new ADT interface around a basic array type in order to control data access and add useful features.

- ❑ The *IndexedList* illustrates the use of the **private** modifier to prevent its data elements and some methods from being accessed outside of the class.

- ❑ Two techniques of flagging errors are shown through *Set()* returning a **boolean** value, and *Get()*, which returns a constructor-specified **int** value.

- ❑ The *Insert()* and *Delete()* methods illustrate more powerful ways of managing array data by opening space for a new value and closing up gaps when a value is removed.

> **Luck is the residue of design.**
> *– Branch Rickey*

Chapter 7: Unordered and Ordered List ADTs

In this chapter, two additional ADTs are presented: the *UnorderedList* and the *OrderedList*. The interfaces of both of these types can be implemented easily using a Java array for storage. This illustrates yet another variation in an interface which can be built around an array structure. The same kind of array used to implement the *IndexedList* discussed in the previous chapter can also be used to implement these very different ADT interfaces.

In both of these ADTs, the ability to access data via an index has been removed entirely, simplifying the interfaces while also reducing the general accessibility of the stored data. Data is stored and retrieved without regard to the index location where it exists in these lists. The advantages offered by these ADTs over a simple array structure are:
 1) simplicity of use, with no indexes to be managed;
 2) built-in display method provided;
 3) for the Ordered List, automatic sorting of the values added.

The interfaces for these ADTs provide identical methods, and differ only in whether their values are ordered when they are stored: the *UnorderedList* always adds new values to the end of the list, while the *OrderedList* adds new values so that the entire list is sorted.

DESIGNING DATA STRUCTURES IN JAVA

Here is the interface description for both ADTs:

The UnorderedList *and* OrderedList *ADTs provide the following capabilities. The constructor determines the total number of entries that can be stored in the List. Values are added to the list using the* Add(value) *method, and deleted using* Remove(value). *The current number of used entries in the list is returned by a call to* Size(), *and the total allocated list capacity is returned by* maxSize(). Find() *returns* **true** *if the value sought is in the list.* Display() *prints out the current contents of the list. The signatures for the methods are as follows:*

    UnorderedList(int capacity) *and* **OrderedList(int capacity)** *– these initialize their respective lists to hold a maximum of* capacity *elements.*

    boolean Add(int value) *– adds* value *to the list if there is room available, and returns* false *only if there was not enough space to add it. The Unordered List adds to the end of the list, the Ordered List adds so that the list is always sorted in ascending order.*

    boolean Remove(int value) *– returns* false *only if* value *was not found in the list, otherwise removes* value *and returns* true.

    int Size() *– returns the current number of items contained in the list.*

    int maxSize() *– returns the total number of items that can be stored in the list. This is determined by the value initially passed to the list constructor.*

    boolean Find(int value) *– returns* **true** *if* value *is in the list.*

    void Display() *– prints out the current contents of the list, with indices.*

As expected, the interface makes no mention of how the lists are to be implemented, and such details are irrelevant at this point.

UNORDERED AND ORDERED LIST ADTS

Example program *main* class

An example main program shows how either the Unordered List or the Ordered List can be used in a main program:

```
 1
 2
 3 public class Main {
 4
 5 public static void main(String[] args) {
```

NOTE: Either version of line 6 can be used below to create either list, since the interface methods are the same for both, even though the behavior differs. Only the constructor parameter of **true** for the ordered version, or **false** for the unordered version, distinguishes the two implementations.

```
 6    OrderedList mylist = new OrderedList(5, true);
OR
 6    OrderedList mylist = new OrderedList(5, false);

 7
 8    //Add 3 new values to the empty mylist
 9    System.out.println("Adding 10, 5, & 7");
10    mylist.Add(10);
11    mylist.Add(5);
12    mylist.Add(7);
13    // Show result
14    mylist.Display();
15
```

Above, three values are added, and the result is displayed.

```
16      // Search for 4, not in the list
17      System.out.println("Value 4 find = "+ mylist.Find(4));
18      // Search for 7, is in the list
19      System.out.println("Value 7 find = "+ mylist.Find(7));
20
```

The search for value 4 will fail, since it was never placed into the list, and the search for 7 will succeed.

```
21      System.out.println("Adding 24 & 3");
22      mylist.Add(24);
23      mylist.Add(3);
24      mylist.Display();
25
26      System.out.println("mylist Size and maxSize: "+
27              mylist.Size()+", "+mylist.maxSize());
28
```

More values are added, and displayed, and the current used and maximum sizes are printed.

```
29      if (!mylist.Add(12))
30          System.out.println("Could not add 12, full");
31
```

The list is full, so 12 cannot be added in the code above.

```
32      System.out.println("Removing 10, adding 12.");
33      mylist.Remove(10);
34      mylist.Add(12);
35      mylist.Display();
36  }
37  }
```

The removal of 10 above allows for the value 12 to be added.

UNORDERED AND ORDERED LIST ADTS

Output of the sample program- *OrderedList* version

The output of the above main program will depend on whether *mylist* is declared to be an Ordered or Unordered List. The output for the *OrderedList* version looks like:

```
run:
Adding 10, 5, & 7
List Contents:
0    5
1    7
2    10
--------------

Value 4 find = false
Value 7 find = true
Adding 24 & 3
List Contents:
0    3
1    5
2    7
3    10
4    24
--------------

mylist Size and maxSize: 5, 5
Could not add 12, full
Removing 10, adding 12.
List Contents:
0    3
1    5
2    7
3    12
4    24
--------------

BUILD SUCCESSFUL (total time: 0 seconds)
```

Output of the sample program- *UnorderedList* version

The output for the *UnorderedList*, using the same *main* program except for the declaration of *mylist* looks like this:

```
run:
Adding 10, 5, & 7
List Contents:
0    10
1    5
2    7
--------------

Value 4 find = false
Value 7 find = true
Adding 24 & 3
List Contents:
0    10
1    5
2    7
3    24
4    3
--------------
```

```
mylist Size and maxSize: 5, 5
Could not add 12, full
Removing 10, adding 12.
List Contents:
0    5
1    7
2    24
3    3
4    12
---------------

BUILD SUCCESSFUL (total time: 0 seconds)
```

Implementing the *OrderedList/UnorderedList* as a class

The Java code for the *OrderedList*, which also implements the *UnorderedList*, follows:

```
1  package orderedlist;
2
3  public class OrderedList {
4     private int length;         // array capacity
5     private int numUsed;        // number slots in use
6     private int[] storage;      // array to hold data
7     private boolean ordered;    // false= not ordered
8
```

All of the data above are private, and not accessible outside of this class.

```
 9    // contructor sets list size and whether ordered
10    public OrderedList(int capacity, boolean useOrder) {
11       length = capacity;
12       storage = new int[length];
13       numUsed = 0;
14       ordered = useOrder;
15    }
16
```

The constructor sets the total number of elements, and also determines whether the *Add()* method will add the value in sorted order or at the end of the list.

```
17    // Adds value to the list if there is room available,
18    // calling either ordered or unordered Add as needed
19    // Returns false if no space to add.
20    public boolean Add(int value) {
21       boolean result = false;
22       if (ordered)
23           result = AddOrdered(value);
24       else
25           result = AddAtEnd(value);
26       return result;
27    }
28
```

Add() is the public method which allows new values to be entered into the list. It uses two private methods to actually do the work, calling the appropriate one based on the *ordered* class data field.

```
29  // Adds value in sorted order, returns false if no room
30  private boolean AddOrdered(int value) {
31      boolean result = false;
32      int index = 0;
33      if (numUsed < length) { // there is room to add
34         // Look for first stored item which is >= value
35         // Stop at end of used slots if no slot is >
36         while ((index < numUsed) &&
37               (storage[index] < value)) {
38            index++;
39         }
40         // index is where new value should go
41         // move everything below index down 1
42         moveItemsDown(index);
43         // save value
44         storage[index] = value;
45         // increase element count
46         numUsed++;
47         result = true;
48      }
49      return result;
50  }
51
```

AddOrdered() first checks that there is room to add a new value, ensuring that *numUsed* is less than *length*. The **while** loop steps through the array, halting either when it gets past the last used item in the array, or when a value >= *value* is found. It then calls *moveItemsDown()* to make space for the new value at the *index* slot, then assigning *value* into the array (line 44). After updating *numUsed* to reflect the newly added value, *result* is returned.

```
52  // Adds at end of list if there is room
53  private boolean AddAtEnd(int value) {
54      boolean result = false;
55      if (numUsed < length) { // there is room to add
56         // save value
57         storage[numUsed] = value;
58         // increase element count
59         numUsed++;
60         result = true;
61      }
62      return result;
63  }
64
65
```

AddAtEnd() first checks that there is room to add a new value, and if so, places the new value into the array at index *numUsed* (recall that this value is always one greater than the highest index in use). After incrementing *numUsed*, *result* is returned.

```
66  // Searches the existing list for value,
67  // and returns the index of the first instance found.
68  // If value is not in the list, returns -1.
69  private int FindIndex(int value) {
70     int result = -1;   //default return
71     int index = 0;
72     boolean found = false;  //set true when match found
73     // search from index 0 through length,
74     //  as long as the value has not been found
75     while ((index < numUsed) && (!found)) {
76         found = (value == storage[index]);
77         if (!found)   //don't increment if value found
78             index++;
79     }
80     // if the value was found, return its index
81     if (found)
82         result = index;
83     return result;
84  }
85
```

The *FindIndex()* method is identical to that defined in the *ArrayUtils* class previously discussed. It is private, and not documented in the ADT interface.

```
86
87  // returns true if value is in the list.
88  public boolean Find(int value) {
89     // use FindIndex, returns true if index not -1
90     return (FindIndex(value) >= 0);
91  }
92
```

Find() is the interfaced search method. It uses *FindIndex()*, and converts its integer result into a boolean value as specified in the ADT interface.

```
 93  // Deletes the existing value located at index in
 94  //   the List by moving the values from index+1
 95  //   through maxLength up 1. False returned only
 96  //   if index is invalid.
 97  //
 98  public boolean Remove(int value) {
 99
100    boolean result = false;   //default return value
101    int location;             //index where value found
102    //find value
103    location = FindIndex(value);
104    // if successful
105    if (location >=0) {
106      moveItemsUp(location);
107      numUsed--;              //update item count
108      result = true;
109    }
110    return result;
111  }
112
```

Remove() deletes the specified *value* by first searching for it using *FindIndex()*. If the index returned in *location* is >=0, *moveItemsUp()* is called to move all lower items up one slot, and *numUsed* is updated to reflect the removal.

```
113  //- Returns the current number of items in the list.
114  public int Size(){
115     return numUsed;
116  }
117
```

Size() returns the current value of *numUsed*.

```
118  // Returns total number of items that can be stored
119  public int maxSize() {
120     return length;
121  }
122
```

maxSize() returns the maximum number of elements that can be stored.

```
123  // Prints out the current contents of the list
124  public void Display() {
125     int index;        //storage array index
126     System.out.println("List Contents:");
127     for (index = 0; index < numUsed; index++){
128          System.out.println(index+"  "+storage[index]);
129     }
130     System.out.println("--------------");
131     System.out.println();
132  }
133
```

Display() prints the array contents with indices in a neat layout.

```
134  // Moves the elements from slot start through length
135  // down to the next higher slot.
136  private void moveItemsDown(int start) {
137     int index;
138     // Must count backwards or all slots = storage[start]
139     for (index = numUsed-1; index >= start; index--){
140          storage[index+1] = storage[index];
141     }
142  }
143
```

```
144 // Moves the elements from slot start through length
145 // up to the next lower indexed slot.
146 private void moveItemsUp(int start) {
147    int index;
148    // Count up, moving values up 1 slot
149    for (index = start; index < numUsed -1; index++){
150        storage[index] = storage[index+1];
151    }
152 }
153
154 }
```

moveItemsDown and *moveItemsDown* are identical to the same methods defined in the *ArrayUtils* class.

UNORDERED AND ORDERED LIST ADTS

Chapter Checklist

❏ The *OrderedList* and *UnorderedList* ADTs described in this chapter demonstrate the important idea that a variety of ADT interfaces can be defined, all built upon the same underlying storage structure, in this case, an array. The example ADTs in previous chapters also used the array, but provided different interfaces.

❏ The *OrderedList* implementation shows how a constructor can be built to accept a boolean parameter which determines how the class will behave. In this case, the *Add()* method was affected, and selected to add values in sorted order or at the end of the list, based on how the class constructor was originally called.

❏ Several **private** methods are used in the class, important in supporting other methods, but invisible to all code which is defined outside of this class. The class breaks complex operations into smaller pieces, and calls methods from within methods to simplify the resulting code.

❏ Several methods from previous chapters make guest appearances in the *OrderedList* class. This shows that some basic array techniques are so useful, and so commonly used, that they are worthy of study and mastery.

DESIGNING DATA STRUCTURES IN JAVA

> It's a poor sort of memory that only
> works backwards.
> - Lewis Carroll

Chapter 8: Sorting

When storing information, it is often important to locate a particular piece of data. Efficient search algorithms depend on organizing the data based on some criteria. A natural approach is to sort the data according to some identifying value. In the case of an integer list or array of data, it is common to place the values in sorted order, as was done with the *OrderedList* ADT.

In the case of the *OrderedList*, the data was maintained in sorted order as it was added to the list. But if an array already contains unsorted data, it is convenient to have algorithms which can rearrange the data into a sorted sequence. This chapter will discuss two sorting algorithms.

The Selection Sort

The Selection Sort is an intuitive algorithm which mimics the process a human being might use when faced with the task of sorting a list of values. As an example, try sorting the following list of values in ascending order, paying particular attention to how you accomplish the task:
    10, 35, 2, 8, 22
Most people look through the list, find the smallest value, write it to a new list,

remove that value from consideration; find the smallest value that is left, write it to the new list, remove that value from the list, and so on, until all the values have been copied to the new list.

The Selection Sort uses a similar algorithm, except that it does not create a new list, but instead exchanges values within the same list, implemented in code as an indexed list, such as an array. In pseudocode, the algorithm, assuming that list indices start at 0 and end at *length*-1, looks like:

> *For **outerindex** = 0 to **length** -2*
>   *For **innerindex** = **outerindex** +1 to **length**-1*
>   *// if smaller value found, move it to top of list*
>   *If **list[innerindex]** < **list[outerindex]***
>   *Swap(**list[innerindex], list[outerindex]**)*

This process compares all the elements in the list array to the first one, exchanging the smaller of the values so that after the first iteration of the outer For loop, the smallest value is in the 0-index slot. On the next loop iteration, slot 0 is ignored, and the list from slot 1 to the end is considered, with the smallest value ending up at slot 1. The process continues until all the values have been compared to each other, and placed into sorted order.

Figures 11 through 15 show the sequence of changes that take place in an example array for each iteration through the outer loop. The ⇨ symbol shows which values are being compared, and the column headings show what exchanges take place. The heading "**a[0]<a[1], OK**" means that no exchange will happen, while "**a[0]>a[2], Swap**" shows that the named slots will exchange values.

SORTING

Array Index	Original Array	a[0]<a[1] OK	a[0]>a[2] Swap	a[0]>a[3] Swap	a[0]>a[4] Swap	a[0]<a[5] OK
0	25	⇨ 25	⇨ ~~25~~ 18	⇨ ~~18~~ 6	⇨ ~~6~~ 3	⇨ 3
1	33	⇨ 33	33	33	33	33
2	18	18	⇨ ~~18~~ 25	25	25	25
3	6	6	6	⇨ ~~6~~ 18	18	18
4	3	3	3	3	⇨ ~~3~~ 6	6
5	12	12	12	12	12	⇨ 12

Figure 11: Selection Sort Example, Pass 1: **outer=0, inner=1..5**

Index	Start 2nd Pass	a[1]>a[2] Swap	a[1]>a[3] Swap	a[1]>a[4] Swap	a[1]<a[5] OK
0	3	3	3	3	3
1	33	⇨ ~~33~~ 25	⇨ ~~25~~ 18	⇨ ~~18~~ 6	⇨ 6
2	25	⇨ ~~25~~ 33	33	33	33
3	18	18	⇨ ~~18~~ 25	25	25
4	6	6	6	⇨ ~~6~~ 18	18
5	12	12	12	12	⇨ 12

Figure 12: Selection Sort Example Pass 2: **outer=1, inner=2..5**

DESIGNING DATA STRUCTURES IN JAVA

Index	Start 3rd Pass	a[2]>a[3] Swap	a[2]>a[4] Swap	a[2]>a[5] Swap
0	3	3	3	3
1	6	6	6	6
2	33	⇨ ~~33~~ 25	⇨ ~~25~~ 18	⇨ ~~18~~ 12
3	25	⇨ ~~25~~ 33	33	33
4	18	18	⇨ ~~18~~ 25	25
5	12	12	12	⇨ ~~12~~ 18

***Figure 13:** Selection Sort Example, Pass 3:* **outer=2, inner=3..5**

Index	Start 4th Pass	a[3]>a[4] Swap	a[3]>a[5] Swap
0	3	3	3
1	6	6	6
2	12	12	12
3	33	⇨ ~~33~~ 25	⇨ ~~25~~ 18
4	25	⇨ ~~25~~ 33	33
5	18	18	⇨ ~~18~~ 25

***Figure 14:** Selection Sort Example, Pass 4:* **outer=3, inner=4..5**

SORTING

Index	Start 5th Pass	a[4]>a[5] Swap
0	3	3
1	6	6
2	12	12
3	18	18
4	33	~~33~~ 25
5	25	~~25~~ 33

Figure 15: *Selection Sort Example, Pass 5:* ***outer=4, inner=5***

Selection Sort Java code

The following code segment implements the Selection Sort algorithm. Its parameters include an integer array, named *array*, a *length* indicating how many elements, starting from index 0, are to be sorted, and a boolean *ascend*, which determines whether the sort will be in ascending or descending order.

```
public static void SelectionSort(int[] array,
                     int length, boolean ascend){
  int outer, inner, temp;
  boolean swap;
  for (outer=0;outer<length-1;outer++)
     for (inner=outer+1;inner<length;inner++)
       {
        if (ascend)
           swap = (array[outer] > array[inner]);
        else
           swap = (array[outer] < array[inner]);
        if (swap)
          {
           temp = array[outer];
           array[outer] = array[inner];
           array[inner] = temp;
          }
       }
  }
```

The *swap* variable is set depending on whether the sort is ascending or descending, which determines whether to compare the values using > or <.

The Bubble Sort

The Bubble Sort algorithm takes a slightly different approach to the sorting task. On each iteration through the loop, pairs of adjacent array slots are compared, and the larger value (for ascending order sorting) "falls" down to the larger index slot. At the end of each outer loop iteration, the largest value in the array is located at the "bottom", in the highest indexed slot being considered.

In pseudocode, the algorithm, is:

> For **outerindex** = **length** -1 downto 1
>   For **innerindex** = **0** to **outerindex**-1
>   // if larger value found, move it down 1 slot
>   If **list[innerindex]** > **list[innerindex+1]**
>   Swap(**list[innerindex], list[innerindex+1]**)

The outer loop counts down, shrinking the number of items considered in the inner loop each time, as the largest value left drops to the bottom of the remaining list. Figures 16 through 20 show the sequence of changes that take place in an example array for each iteration through the outer loop, using the same notation as was used for the Selection Sort example.

Array Index	Original Array	a[0]<a[1] OK	a[1]>a[2] Swap	a[2]>a[3] Swap	a[3]>a[4] Swap	a[4]>a[5] Swap
0	25	⇨ 25	25	25	25	25
1	33	⇨ 33	⇨ 33̶ 18	18	18	18
2	18	18	⇨ 18̶ 33	⇨ 33̶ 6	6	6
3	6	6	6	⇨ 6̶ 33	⇨ 33̶ 3	3
4	3	3	3	3	⇨ 3̶ 33	⇨ 33̶ 12
5	12	12	12	12	12	⇨ 12̶ 33

Figure 16: Bubble Sort Example, Pass 1: **outer=5, inner=0..4**

Index	Start 2nd Pass	a[0]>a[1] Swap	a[1]>a[2] Swap	a[2]>a[3] Swap	a[3]>a[4] Swap
0	25	~~25~~ 18	18	18	18
1	18	~~18~~ 25	~~25~~ 6	6	6
2	6	6	~~6~~ 25	~~25~~ 3	3
3	3	3	3	~~3~~ 25	~~25~~ 12
4	12	12	12	12	~~12~~ 25
5	33	33	33	33	33

Figure 17: Bubble Sort Example Pass 2: **outer=4, inner=0..3**

Index	Start 3rd Pass	a[0]>a[1] Swap	a[1]>a[2] Swap	a[2]>a[3] Swap
0	18	~~18~~ 6	6	6
1	6	~~6~~ 18	~~18~~ 3	3
2	3	3	~~3~~ 18	~~18~~ 12
3	12	12	12	~~12~~ 18
4	25	25	25	25
5	33	33	33	33

Figure 18: Bubble Sort Example, Pass 3: **outer=3, inner=0..2**

SORTING

Index	Start 4th Pass	a[0]>a[1] Swap	a[1]<a[2] OK
0	6	⇨ 6̶ 3	3
1	3	⇨ 3̶ 6	⇨ 6
2	12	12	⇨ 12
3	18	18	18
4	25	25	25
5	33	33	33

Figure 19: *Bubble Sort Example, Pass 4:* ***outer=2, inner=0..1***

Index	Start 5th Pass	a[0]<a[1] OK
0	3	⇨ 3
1	6	⇨ 6
2	12	12
3	18	18
4	25	25
5	33	33

Figure 20: *Bubble Sort Example, Pass 5:* ***outer=1, inner=0***

Bubble Sort Java code

The Bubble Sort code below takes the same parameters as the Selection Sort code. algorithm, and uses them in the same manner.

```
public static void BubbleSort(int[] array, int length,
                                         boolean ascend){
  int outer, inner, temp;
  boolean swap;
  for (outer=length-1;outer>=1;outer--)
     for (inner=0;inner< outer;inner++)
        {
         if (ascend)
            swap = (array[inner] > array[inner+1]);
         else
            swap = (array[inner] < array[inner+1]);
         if (swap)
            {
             temp = array[inner];
             array[inner] = array[inner+1];
             array[inner+1] = temp;
            }
        }
}
```

The outer loop counts down, as mentioned earlier, shortening the length of the list which the inner loop will consider on each iteration. The *ascend* and *swap* variables work the same as in the Selection Sort code.

SORTING

Chapter Checklist

❏ Sorting is a common need when organizing data so that individual items in a list can be found more easily.

❏ The Selection Sort is an intuitive algorithm which mimics the method people use to manually sort a list of values. The goal on each iteration through the outer loop is to move the smallest value in the remaining unsorted part of the list to the lowest indexed position.

❏ The Bubble Sort uses a different approach, comparing adjacent pairs of list slots, allowing the largest value to fall to the bottom of the list. On each outer loop iteration, the remaining unsorted part of the list is tested to move the largest value to the end of that section.

DESIGNING DATA STRUCTURES IN JAVA

> True genius resides in the capacity
> for evaluation of uncertain, hazardous,
> and conflicting information.
> – *Winston Churchill*

Chapter 9: Evaluating Algorithms

The world of computer science includes a branch devoted to the study of algorithms and their relative efficiencies. For any given problem, there may be multiple algorithmic solutions. Selecting the **best** algorithm is not always an obvious choice, and there are many different criteria which could be used in the evaluation process. One measure might be the simplicity and ease of understanding the algorithm. Another measure considers the amount of memory and disk storage required. Measuring speed of execution is another possible criterion.

Engineering a solution to a problem often involves trade-offs, because it is uncommon to be able to optimize every aspect of a design. One common dilemma is the choice between *maximizing speed* and *minimizing memory usage*– usually, only one of these objectives can be attained at a time. Optimization deals with analyzing the relationships among the list of design objectives (remember those *software requirements* from Chapter 1?), and determining the degree to which they are actually and simultaneously attainable. This is usually not a simple task.

Evaluating Time Efficiency Using *Big-O Notation*

This chapter focuses on just one aspect of algorithm analysis, *time efficiency*. The objective of the analysis will be to assign a machine- and language-independent classification to an algorithm so that its efficiency can be compared with other algorithms. Of necessity, our description is intended to provide a brief and high-level introduction to a complex field of study.

The characterization used here is named *Big-O notation*. In computer science, it is a means of classifying the upper-bound (or worst-case) time behavior of an algorithm. This is defined by estimating the relationship between the number of inputs to the algorithm and the amount of processing time the algorithm requires.

As an example, both the Selection Sort and Bubble Sort algorithms are characterized as **O(n^2)** time complexity. This means that as **n**, the number of items in the array, goes up, the time for sorting the list goes up by the **n^2**. To put it another way, if the time to process **n** items is defined as time **T**, then if **n** is doubled, the time will go up to **4T**, and if **n** is multiplied by **10**, then the time will go up to **100T**. Even though both of these sort algorithms have nested loops where one executes **n** times, and the other executes 1 less time on each iteration, the overall behavior is classified as bounded by **O(n^2)**.

A Comparison of *Big-O* Functions

Figure 21 is a table of some common functions of n, illustrating their differing growth rates. For comparison purposes, the functions **$log_{10}(n)$, $log_2(n)$, n^2, n^3, 2^n, $n!$,** and **n^n** were chosen because they are relatively common in algorithm analysis. These are shown in the table columns, ordered according to increasing rate of growth. Some of the results may be startling to the uninitiated.

The **$log_{10}(n)$** and **$log_2(n)$** functions increase the most slowly. For example, between **n** = 50 and **n** = 100, **$log_{10}(n)$** increases from **1.699** to **2.000** and **$log_2(n)$** goes from **5.644** to **6.644**. Qualitatively, a logarithmic function exhibits a relatively *small* increase when there is a *large* increase in **n**. In the table's middle columns, the **n^2** and **n^3** functions show large increases over the same range of **n** from **50** to **100**. In the big picture, computer scientists tend to regard Big-O complexities involving simple powers of **n** as challenging, but manageable classes of algorithms.

At the other end of the spectrum, again with **n** of **50** and **100**, the function **2^n** increases from about 10^{15} to 10^{30}, an amazing increase, and **n!** (that is, **n-factorial**) goes from 10^{64} to 10^{157}. An even faster increase occurs with the **n^n** function, where the results go from the ridiculously large value of 10^{84} to the inconceivably large (and adverbially challenging) 10^{200} which, in layman's terms, is "really, **really, _really_** big."

n	$log_{10}(n)$	$log_2(n)$	n^2	n^3	2^n	n!	n^n
1	0.000	0.000	1	1	2	1	1
2	0.301	1.000	4	8	4	2	4
3	0.477	1.585	9	27	8	6	27
4	0.602	2.000	16	64	16	24	256
5	0.699	2.322	25	125	32	120	3125
6	0.778	2.585	36	216	64	720	46656
7	0.845	2.807	49	343	128	5040	823543
8	0.903	3.000	64	512	256	40320	1.6×10^7
9	0.954	3.170	81	729	512	362880	3.8×10^8
10	1.000	3.322	100	1000	1024	3628800	1.0×10^{10}
20	1.301	4.322	400	8000	1048576	2.4×10^{18}	1.0×10^{26}
30	1.477	4.907	900	27000	1.0×10^9	2.6×10^{32}	2.0×10^{44}
50	1.699	5.644	2500	125000	1.1×10^{15}	3.0×10^{64}	8.8×10^{84}
100	2.000	6.644	10000	1000000	1.2×10^{30}	9.3×10^{157}	1.0×10^{200}

Figure 21: *Table of values for various common functions of* **n**

Big-O Estimation and Polynomial Functions

Big-O notation is not intended to be a precise estimate of algorithmic time complexity. Instead, it is a large-scale, gross estimate of time behavior as **n** changes. For example, suppose a detailed analysis of three different algorithms, A, B, and C, determines that each has a time function represented by a polynomial, as follows:

Algorithm A time: $5n^3 + 2n^2 + 4n + 50$

Algorithm B time: $n^3 + 100$

Algorithm C time: $12n^3 + 36n$

These three examples all have a Big-O complexity of **O(n^3)**, because in Big-O estimation:
    1) all constant values not involving **n** are ignored,
    2) all coefficients of **n** are ignored, and
    3) only the highest power of **n** is considered, ignoring all lower powers

Although it may appear that this method of estimation is overly coarse, there is a justification for ignoring these otherwise significant numeric elements of the polynomial. As **n** becomes substantially large, the importance of those ignored elements become less and less significant, and only the most rapidly increasing term in the polynomial is considered. This type of characterization is sufficient to allow algorithms to be compared and ranked relative to each other.

EVALUATING ALGORITHMS

Chapter Checklist

❏ It is useful to compare the efficiency of algorithms in order to determine whether they are acceptable or appropriate in fulfilling the requirements of a particular project.

❏ Various criteria could be used in evaluating an algorithm, such as: ease of understanding, simplicity of implementation, data storage requirements, and speed of execution. Big-O notation will be used to estimate speed of execution (or *time complexity*) of an algorithm, relative to **n**, the number of inputs or items to be processed.

❏ Functions of **n** commonly considered in algorithm evaluation include logarithmic functions such as **$log_{10}(n)$** and **$log_2(n)$** which increase relatively slowly; **n^2** and **n^3** which increase quickly, but can often be managed; and the explosive **2^n, n!,** and **n^n** functions which are considered to be intractable for all but the smallest values of **n**.

❏ Big-O notation estimates the upper-bound of an algorithm's time complexity. It simplifies the actual mathematical expression for the execution time function by ignoring constants, coefficients, and lower-order functions of **n**, and looks only at the most quickly increasing term of the expression.

DESIGNING DATA STRUCTURES IN JAVA

> Ask, and it shall be given you;
> seek, and ye shall find;
> knock, and it shall be opened unto you.
> – *Jesus of Nazareth*

Chapter 10: Binary Searches

Searching stored data to find a value is one of the most common tasks performed by a computer. Whether it is an internet text search, or finding whether or not a person's information is located in a particular database, computers are able to perform searches through vast collections of data in ways that an individual person could never possibly complete in a lifetime. The efficiency of such searches is important, even for high-speed computers, when either the amount of data to be examined, or the number of searches to be done, or both, is large.

The Linear Search

The simple and obvious approach to searching an array of data is to start at the beginning, and check every element until the value being sought is found, or all the elements have been checked. This is known as a Linear Search, and if there are *n* items in the array, on average it will take *n/2* comparisons to find an item that is actually in the array, or worst case, *n* comparisons if the item is not in the list. This translates, in Big-O form, to **O(n)** time complexity. Although this function is not unreasonable, searching vast amounts of data will still take a long time to complete. If the data is not organized in any way, there is no alternative except looking everywhere until the item is found, or all possibilities have been exhausted.

The Binary Search

People are familiar with another, intuitive search approach when the data to be searched is ordered. For example, consider the 'high-low guessing game': person #1 thinks of a number, and announces the range ("My number is between 1 and 100"), person #2 tries to guess the number, and for each guess, person #1 tells whether the guess is correct, too-high, or too-low. It would not be wise or efficient to attempt a Linear search..."Is it 1?", "Is it 2?", "Is it 3?", et cetera. Instead, it is intuitive to begin with a guess in the middle of the range, and repeatedly adjust the range of guesses offered, cutting the range in half based on the too-high and too-low responses, until the number is correctly guessed ("Is it 50?", "Too high", "Is it 25?", "Too low", "Is it 37?", "I just changed the number.").

The high-low game example demonstrates a Binary Search, so named because at each iteration, the size of the search space is halved, ultimately narrowing the search to a single element. This can be accomplished in a computer program by storing the data in an array, and progressively sub-dividing the portion of the array being searched until the value is found, or there is only one element remaining to be checked.

The one important requirement of the Binary Search is that the data must be sorted before the search can take place. Having the data sorted on the value being searched for allows the algorithm to tell what action to take once it is determined that a value being examined is either too-high or too-low compared to the middle of the current search interval.

A Binary Search is considerably more efficient than the Linear search, providing a **$O(\log_2 n)$** time complexity. This means that doubling the number of items searched only increases the number of comparisons required by 1.

Binary Search Code

The following Java code implements a Binary Search algorithm.

```
// Binary search looks through 0..(length-1) elements
// of the array, using subdivision to find the element
// in O(log(n)) time

 1  public static int BinarySearch(int value, int[] array,
                                        int length){
 2    int high, low, mid, result;
 3    boolean found;
 4    result = -1; //default return value
 5    low = 0;
 6    high = length-1;
 7    mid = (high-low) / 2 + low;
 8    found = (array[mid]== value);
 9    while ((high > (low)) &&(! found)) {
10      if (value < array[mid])
11         high = mid-1;
12      else
13         low = mid+1;
14      mid = (high-low) / 2  + low;
15      found = (array[mid]== value);
16    } //while
17    if (found)
18      result = mid;
19
20    return result;
21  }
```

BinarySearch takes three parameters: *value*, the value being sought, *array*, the list of data, and *length*, the number of values in the array to be searched. Two variables, *low* and *high,* are used to define the range of the array to be considered at each iteration of the search. Initially, *low* is 0 (line 5), and *high* is set to the highest index to be searched, *length-1* (line 6). The middle of the range is maintained in *mid,* initially at line 7, and later, inside the loop, at line 14, where it is set to the index halfway between *low* and *high.* Boolean *found* is set at lines 8 and 15 with the result of the comparison of *array[mid]* with *value.* The **while** loop (line 9) condition specifies that the loop will end when the value is found, or when *high* becomes <= *low*, indicating that the searchable interval has dropped to at most one already-compared element, and no further search is possible. The **if** at line 10 sets *high* to *mid-1* if *value* must be in the lower half of the current interval, or otherwise updates *low* to *mid+1* to search the upper half of the interval. Finally, line 18 updates *result* from its default failure value to the found location if the search was successful.

Array Index	1 Finding 47 A[4]<47 LOW Up	2 A[6]<47 LOW Up	3 A[7]=47 FOUND
0	LOW ⇨ 1	1	1
1	4	4	4
2	11	11	11
3	16	16	16
4	MID ⇨ 35	35	35
5	40	LOW ⇨ 40	40
6	45	MID ⇨ 45	45
7	47	47	LOW, MID ⇨ 47
8	HIGH ⇨ 48	HIGH ⇨ 48	HIGH ⇨ 48

Table 10-1: Binary Search on 9-element array

BINARY SEARCHES

Table 10-1 illustrates a binary search for the value 47 in a 9-element array. Column 1 shows the initial configuration. Tracing the activity through the code, *low* is set to 0, *high* is set to 8, and *mid* is initialized to 4 (lines 5-7). *found* is **false** because *a[4]* != 47 (line 8). The **while** loop is entered, and *a[4]* is less than 47, so line 13 executes, setting *low* to *mid+1*, or 5, *mid* is set to ((8-5)/2 + 5) = 6, and *found* remains **false** (line 15). *high* > *low* is **true**, so the **while** continues (table column 2). Since *a[6]* is less than 47, *low* gets (6+1) = 7, and *mid* is set to ((8-7)/2+7) = 7 (same as *low*). *found* becomes **true** as *a[7]* == *47* is **true** (column 3), causing the **while** loop to terminate. In comparison with a linear search, which would have taken eight comparisons, for indices 0 through 7, the binary search required only three tests of *a[mid]* to find the value 47.

Chapter Checklist

❑ A Linear Search simply checks every element until either the sought value is found, or every element has been tried. It has **O(n)** time complexity, and is the only option available if the data is not ordered in some way.

❑ The Binary Search is more efficient than the Linear Search, but requires that the data is sorted based on the value being sought. On each iteration, the number of items to be check is halved, resulting in **O(log$_2$n)** time complexity.

❑ The array-based code for the Binary Search is straightforward, and moves *low, mid,* and *high* index values around to progressively shrink the portion of the array where the value being searched for might be located.

> The want-to-be composer defying convention isn't innovative; he is lazy...because he hasn't yet learned the traditions of his craft.
> – *The Complete Idiot's Guide to Writing Poetry*
> *By Nikki Moustaki*

Chapter 11: The Stack ADT

The Stack ADT is a standard data type in computer science, with a conventional, agreed-upon interface which specifies its functionality and methods. Because it has a known definition, any significant deviations from this Stack specification, such as changing the method names, is strongly discouraged. It is possible to invent a Stack-like ADT for a specific purpose, with custom features, but a programmer would be wise to name the new ADT in such a way that it could not be confused with the conventional Stack definition.

The Stack Interface

The standard Stack interface is described as follows:

A Stack is a **Last In, First Out (LIFO)** *structure which allows items to be added and removed from the same end of the list, which is designated as the* **Top** *of the Stack. Items are removed in the reverse of the sequence in which they were added. The Stack interface provides the following methods:*

push(int x)- *adds the value* x *to the top of the Stack.*

int pop()- *removes and returns value of the top Stack item, if there is one.*

int top()- *returns the value of the top Stack item, if there is one, without removal.*

int size()- *returns the number of items currently in the Stack.*

boolean isEmpty()- *returns* ***true*** *if there are no items in the Stack.*

For example, if the values **1, 6, 5, 4** *are pushed onto the Stack, a sequence of pop operations will return* **4, 5, 6, 1** *, in that order.*

The Stack purposely limits all access to its data, allowing only the push(), pop(), *and* top() *methods to add, remove, and view data. For example, there is no way to see the third item from the top, except by first removing the items located above it on the Stack.*

Real-World Examples of Stacks

The idea of a Stack is common in everyday life. Some examples are:

    1) a cafeteria plate dispenser, which holds a stack of plates in a spring-loaded, cylindrical tube such that only the top plate is available to be removed;

    2) a restaurant napkin dispenser allowing only the outermost napkin to be removed;

    3) putting batteries into and out of a traditional 2-cell flashlight;

    4) multiple cars parked in a single-car-wide driveway;

    5) web browser BACK history buttons, where each click moves to the most

THE STACK ADT

recent previous page (but the FORWARD button sort of violates the Stack's one-direction access concept...);

    6) the computer mechanism that allows a method to call a method which calls another method, etc, and then unwind the sequence backwards, as each method completes execution and returns to its caller.

Using the Stack ADT

One of the advantages of the ADT concept is that the structure can be used by a programmer having no information about ADT's inner workings. As an example, the following method uses a character version of a Stack to reverse the contents of a String:

```
 1  public static String reverse(String s){
 2     CharStack cstack = new CharStack(50);
 3     String temp= "";
 4     int i;
 5     for (i=0;i<s.length();i++){
 6        cstack.push(s.charAt(i));
 7     }
 8     for (i=0;i<s.length();i++){
 9        temp = temp +(cstack.pop());
10     }
11     return temp;
12  }
```

Simply understanding what a Stack is, and how it behaves, is sufficient to be able to program this simple method. After declaring and initializing the CharStack *cstack* at line 2, the String *temp* is created as an empty string. The **for** loop (lines 5-7) steps through each character in the parameter String *s*, pushing them onto *cstack*. The following loop (8-10) pops the characters off *cstack*, and concatenates each one onto *temp* , in the reverse order that they appeared in *s,* and finally, *temp* is returned.

An example use of the *reverse* method looks like:

```
System.out.println(reverse("This string is backwards"));
```

and produces the printed output:

```
sdrawkcab si gnirts sihT
```

The key idea here is the ability to use an ADT simply based on its interface description, without any implementation details.

Stack Implementation Using Java Code

The following code implements the Stack ADT using an array for storage:

```
1  package stackqueue;
2
3  // Implements a stack ADT using an array for storage
4  public class Stack {
5      private int[] storage;
6      private int top; //always the index of the top item
7
```

There are no **public** data fields for the Stack. The array for *storage* and the **int** for the *top* index are only accessible within this class. The topmost item is always at the index stored in *top*.

```
8      //Constructor sets size of array
9      public Stack(int n){
10         storage = new int[n];
11         top = -1;
12     }
13
```

THE STACK ADT

The constructor accepts a parameter specifying the maximum number of elements allowed in the Stack, and initializes *top* to the chosen "empty" condition.

```
14      //push adds value to top of stack
15      public void push(int value){
16          if (top < (storage.length-1)){
17              top++;
18              storage[top] = value;
19          }
20      }
21
```

The *push()* method checks to see if there is any more room to add, and if so, moves *top* up one slot, and assigns the new value at that array slot.

```
22      //pop removes the top item, updates top
23      public int pop(){
24          int result = -1;
25          if (! isEmpty()) {
26              result = storage[top];
27              top--;
28          }
29          return result;
30      }
31
```

pop() checks to see if there is any data in the Stack, and, if so, sets *result* to the value located at the array slot indicated by *top*. *top* is then decremented, and *result* is returned. If there is nothing in the Stack, *pop()* returns -1.

```
32      //top returns top item only, no removal
33      public int top(){
34          int result = -1;
35          if (! isEmpty()) {
36              result = storage[top];
37          }
38          return result;
39      }
40
```

top() checks to see if there is any data in the Stack, and, if so, sets *result* to the value located at the array slot indicated by *top*, without changing *top*, so that the data in the Stack is unchanged. Then, *result* is returned. If there is nothing in the Stack, *top()* returns -1.

```
41      //size is number of elements in the stack
42      public int size(){
43          return (top + 1);
44      }
45
```

size() simply returns *top+1*. If the Stack is empty, this will return 0, as expected.

```
46      //isEmpty is true when there are no items
47      public boolean isEmpty() {
48          return top < 0;
49      }
50
```

isEmpty() returns **true** only when *top* is -1 (the only negative value it can ever hold), indicating there are no items in the Stack.

THE STACK ADT

```
51    //prints the stack contents
52    public void display(){
53       int i;
54       //label top of stack
55       System.out.print("TOP <- |");
56          //allow special empty handling
57          if (!isEmpty()) {
58             i=top;
59             while (i >= 0){
60                System.out.print(storage[i]+"|");
61                i--;
62             }
63          }
64          else //display empty message
65             System.out.print("empty|");
66          //label rear of queue
67          System.out.println();
68    }
69 }
```

Not specified in the Stack ADT, the *display()* method is provided as a convenience, printing out the Stack values in a neat output like:

```
TOP <-  |8|7|6|5|
```

Example Operation of the Stack

A simple illustration of the array-based Stack in operation is shown in Figures 22 through 25. Figure 22 shows the Stack in its initial state, with defaulted 0 values in the array, and *top* set to -1, the empty indicator. Figure 23 shows the result of the call *push(5)*, and the movement of *top* to 0. In Figure 24, successive calls of *push(8)*, *push(2)*, *push(11)* have moved *top* to 3. Finally, Figure 25 shows the result of calls *pop()*, *pop()*, moving *top* back down to index 1. Note that the data that is popped off of the Stack need not be erased, it simply will not be accessible through the Stack interface, and may be disregarded.

Index	Stack Array
5	0
4	0
3	0
2	0
1	0
0	0

Figure 22: Array-Based Stack Empty, **TOP = -1**

Index	Stack Array
5	0
4	0
3	0
2	0
1	0
⇨ 0	5

Figure 23: Array-Based Stack After push(5), **TOP = 0**

Index	Stack Array
5	0
4	0
⇨ 3	11
2	2
1	8
0	5

Figure 24: Array-Based Stack Following push(8), push(2), push(11), **TOP = 3**

Index	Stack Array
5	0
4	0
3	11
2	2
⇨ 1	8
0	5

Figure 25: Array-Based Stack Following pop(), pop() **TOP = 1**

THE STACK ADT

Chapter Checklist

❏ A Stack is a recognized, fundamental ADT and data structure in computer science. Everyday real-world examples include physical stacks of plates and batteries placed into the tube of a 2-cell flashlight.

❏ The Stack behaves as a LIFO (Last-in, First-Out) structure.

❏ The recognized interface for the Stack includes the *push()*, *pop()*, *top()*, *size()*, and *isEmpty()* methods.

❏ Using just the ADT interface definition, without implementation details, useful programs can be written using Stacks.

DESIGNING DATA STRUCTURES IN JAVA

> All right everyone, line up alphabetically
> according to your height.
> – *Casey Stengel*

Chapter 12: The Queue ADT

The Queue ADT, like the Stack, is a recognized, standard data structure in computer science, and when implemented, should comply with the interface described.

The Queue Interface

The standard Queue interface:

*A Queue is a **First In, First Out (FIFO)** structure, in which items are always added at one end, called the **Rear**, and always removed from the other end, called the **Front**. The sequence in which items were added is maintained when they are removed from the Queue. The Queue interface provides the following methods:*

    insert(int x)- *adds the value x to the rear of the Queue.*

    int remove()- *removes and returns value of the front Queue item, if there is one.*

    int front()- *returns the value of the front Queue item, if there is one, without removal.*

    int size()- *returns the number of items currently in the Queue.*

boolean isEmpty()- *returns* **true** *if there are no items in the Queue.*

For example, if the values **1, 6, 5, 4** *are inserted into the Queue, a sequence of remove operations will return* **1, 6, 5, 4** *, in the same order that they were added.*

The Queue purposely limits all access to its data, allowing only the insert(), remove(), *and* front() *methods to add, remove, or view data. For example, there is no way to see the third item from the front, except by first removing the items located in front of it in the Queue.*

Real-World Examples of Queues

The idea of a Queue is simple, and corresponds to a line of people waiting in line at a checkout stand... but with no *cutting in line* allowed. The primary idea of the queue is to maintain the original sequence of the elements so that they depart the queue in the same order that they arrived. A time-ordered list of tasks to be performed, or a sequence of interdependent steps in a process, where order must be enforced, are additional examples.

THE QUEUE ADT

Using the Queue ADT

Suppose a utility is needed to reverse the contents of a Queue. Again, using just the ADT interface, the Queue can be used in a program, knowing nothing about its implementation. Here is a method which reverses the elements in a Queue by pushing them onto a Stack, then popping them back into the Queue. The net effect is that the elements are now in the reverse sequence from their original locations in the Queue:

```
1    public static void reverseQ(Queue q) {
2       Stack s = new Stack(q.size());
3       while (!q.isEmpty())
4          s.push(q.remove());
5       while (!s.isEmpty())
6          q.insert(s.pop());
7    }
```

This code is incredibly simple, and requires no implementation details about either the Stack or the Queue. The Queue elements are pushed into the Stack in the first **while** loop, and the process is reversed in the second, removing from the Stack and re-inserting into the Queue, leaving the Queue in the desired configuration.

An example use of the *reverseQ* method is:

```
reverseQ(q);
```

where *q* is a previously declared and used Queue. The power of a well-defined ADT interface is of great value in solving a problem without having to 'reinvent the wheel' every time a similar structure is needed.

Queue Implementation Using Java Code

The following code implements the Stack ADT using an array for storage:

```
1  package stackqueue;
2  // Implements a queue ADT using an array for storage
3  public class Queue {
4      private int capacity;   //maximum number of elements
5      private int[] storage;
6      private int front, rear;
7      private boolean empty; //true if no elements;
8
```

There are no **public** data fields for the Queue. The array is used for *storage* and **int** values keep track of the total *capacity* of the Queue, as well as the indices for the *front* and *rear* of the Queue. A **boolean** *empty* is set true whenever there are no elements left in the Queue.

```
9       //Initialize queue to have size elements at most
10      public Queue(int size){
11          capacity = size;
12          storage = new int[capacity];
13          front = 0;
14          rear = -1;
15          empty = true;
16      }
17
```

The constructor accepts a parameter specifying the maximum number of elements allowed in the Queue, and initializes *front* to 0, *rear* to -1, which is the inital 'empty' situation. *capacity* is set to the array size, and *empty* is set **true**.

THE QUEUE ADT

```
18      //Add value to rear of queue
19      //   with wrap-around
20      public void insert(int value){
21          //if there is room to add
22          if (size()< capacity){
23             // move rear up, wrap to 0 at end
24             rear++;
25             if (rear == capacity){
26                rear = 0;
27             }
28             storage[rear] = value;
29             //there is at least one element
30             empty = false;
31          }
32      }
33
```

The *insert()* method checks to see if there is any more room to add, by comparing the current *size()* to the total *capacity*, and if so, moves *rear* up one slot. If *rear* exceeds the largest allowed array index, it is wrapped-back to 0, to reuse the space. Finally, new value is added at the *rear* array slot, and *empty* is set to **false**.

```
34          //return and remove front queue element
35          public int remove(){
36              //save the return value
37              int result = storage[front];
38              //move front up, wrap to 0 at end
39              front++;
40              if (front == capacity)
41                 front = 0;
42              //** front was just incremented; must
43              //identify empty condition where front is
44              // 'just ahead of' rear, to distinguish
45              // from full condition- if front is now rear+1
46              // OR (front is 0 and rear is capacity-1)
47              empty = ((front == rear + 1) ||
                          ((front==0)&&(rear==(capacity-1))));
48              return result;
49          }
50
```

remove() assumes there is data in the stack, and should only be called after a call to *isEmpty()* is used to verify this. *result* gets the value located at the array slot indicated by *front*. *front* is then incremented, with a wrap-around check to set it back to 0 if it exceeds the largest array index. Since *front* has just changed, the empty Queue situation is checked to see if *front* is now in the slot following *rear*. This can occur in two ways, as shown in the conditions at line 47. Finally, *result* is returned.

```
51          //return, but don't remove, front element
52          public int front(){
53              //save the return value
54              return storage[front];
55          }
56
```

front() returns the array slot at the *front* index, without any error check, so *isEmpty()* should be called first, to verify there is data in the Queue. *front* is left unaltered.

THE QUEUE ADT

```
57        //Returns number of elements currently in queue
58        public int size(){
59            int result;
60            int gap; //unused space between rear, front
61                     // when rear < front
62            //empty tracks whether no elements
63            if (empty)
64               result = 0;
65            else //can use formula to calculate #
66              {
67               //if wrap has not happened
68               if (rear >= front)
69                  result = rear-front+1;
70               else //rear is < front, find gap between
71                 {
72                   //gap is # unused slots in between
73                   gap = front - rear - 1;
74                   //used slots = capacity - unused
75                   result = capacity - gap;
76                 }
77              }
78           return result;
79         }
80
```

size() returns the number of elements in the Queue, but because of the wrap around design, it must check three different conditions in order to determine this. First, if *empty* is true, the result is 0. This is needed because having *front* directly ahead of *rear* can mean either that the Queue is empty, or that it is full– there is no way to distinguish this as implemented, except for setting *empty* in the *remove()* method, when the last item is removed. If the Queue is not empty, then if *rear* is a higher index than *front,* the number of elements is just their difference, plus 1 (line 69). However, if wrap around has occurred, and *rear* is less than *front,* the gap of free slots between them is found (line 73), and the result is the *capacity* less the *gap* (free slots, line 75).

```
81      //true if no elements
82      public boolean isEmpty(){
83          return size() == 0;
84      }
85
```

isEmpty() returns **true** only when *size()* returns 0.

```
86      //prints the queue contents
87      public void display(){
88          int i;
89          //label front of queue
90          System.out.print("FRONT <- |");
91          //allow special empty handling
92          if (!isEmpty()) {
93            i=front;
94            while (i != rear){
95               System.out.print(storage[i]+"|");
96               i++;
97               if (i == capacity)
98                  i=0;
99            }
100           System.out.print(storage[rear]+"|");
101         }
102         else //display empty message
103           System.out.print("empty|");
104         //label rear of queue
105         System.out.println(" <- REAR");
106     }
107 }
108
```

THE QUEUE ADT

Not specified in the Queue ADT, the *display()* method is provided as a convenience, printing out the Queue values in a neat output like:

```
FRONT <- |5|6|7|8| <- REAR
```

Example Operation of the Queue

A simple illustration of the array-based Queue in operation is shown in Figures 26 through 29. Figure 26 shows the Queue in its initial state, with defaulted 0 values in the array, *rear* set to -1, and *front* set to 0. Figure 27 shows the result of the call *insert(5)*, and the movement of *rear* to 0. In Figure 28, successive calls of *insert(8)*, *insert(2)*, *insert(11)* have moved *rear* to 3, while *front* is still 0. Finally, Figure 29 shows the result of calls *remove()*, *remove()*, moving *front* up twice, to 2, the current front item of the Queue. As in the Stack, the data that is removed is simply ignored, and remains inaccessible to the Queue's interfaced methods.

Index	Queue Array
5	0
4	0
3	0
2	0
1	0
0	0

Figure 26: Array-Based Queue Empty, **REAR= -1, FRONT=0**

Index	Queue Array
5	0
4	0
3	0
2	0
1	0
F,R ⇨ 0	5

Figure 27: Array-Based Queue After insert(5), **REAR=0, FRONT= 0**

Index	Queue Array
5	0
4	0
R⇨ 3	11
2	2
1	8
F⇨ 0	5

Figure 28: *Array-Based Queue Following insert(8), insert(2), insert(11),* **REAR= 3, FRONT=0**

Index	Queue Array
5	0
4	0
R⇨ 3	11
F⇨ 2	2
1	8
0	5

Figure 29: *Array-Based Queue Following remove(), remove(),* **REAR=3, FRONT=2**

THE QUEUE ADT

Chapter Checklist

- ❏ A Queue is another basic, defined ADT and data structure in computer science. Real-world examples are a line waiting for service, or a sequential list of tasks to be performed.

- ❏ The Queue behaves as a FIFO (First-in, First-Out) structure.

- ❏ The recognized interface for the Queue includes the *insert()*, *remove()*, *front()*, *size()*, and *isEmpty()* methods.

- ❏ Using just the ADT interface definition, without implementation details, useful programs can be written using Queues and Stacks.

DESIGNING DATA STRUCTURES IN JAVA

> **Reason's last step is the recognition that there are an infinite number of things which are beyond it.**
> *– Blaise Pascal, "Pensées" (1670)*

Chapter 13: The Dynamic Linked List

A Dynamic Linked List is a common programming data structure. It is called *Dynamic* because the contents and size of the list can be modified dynamically at runtime, allocating and deallocating memory space as needed. The *Linked* adjective means that the list is constructed such that the list elements have one or more references or pointers to other elements, thus linking them together. New elements can be allocated to hold more data, and unused elements can be removed from the list, and returned to the program's available memory.

Foundations– the Node Class

Linked Lists are made up of individual objects which form the containers used to store each piece of data. First, consider the following Node class definition:

```
public class Node {
    int data;
    Node next;

    public Node(int value, Node nxt){
        data = value;
        next = nxt;
    }
}
```

One odd feature should be apparent after perusing this Node class: it contains a self-referencing Node variable in its data fields! At first glance, this may seem illegal, for how can a Node object *contain* a Node object? Wouldn't this set up some infinite looping if an attempt is made to allocate a Node using **new**?

The answer is, the Node class is perfectly acceptable, and causes no problems when allocating an object. This makes sense, because a class reference is simply a reference (or an address) of an object, and is *not* the object itself. In fact, an important idea to remember regarding reference variables is this: **all Java object reference variables are the *same size (i.e., the same number of bytes), no matter how much space the object requires.*** References can be thought of as a **long** integer type, which is conceptually the starting address of the object to which they refer. This means that when the Java compiler sees any object reference, such as any of these:

```
Node next;
int[] xarray;
String name;
```

it is able to determine exactly how much space is needed for each, namely 'one reference variable's worth' of memory. This is true no matter how large the object allocated turns out to be. Even if the class has a reference variable of its own type, the compiler is able to set aside a fixed, standard amount of space for it.

Although this text consistently uses the terms 'node' and the Node class for the elements making up a Linked List, the term is arbitrary. Java does not have a *Node* reserved word, and the programmer is free to name such a class in any way they wish. For example:

```
public class ListItem {
    int data;
    ListItem nextitem;
    . . .
```

would be another acceptable way to construct a Linked List element.

Connecting Nodes Together

The next step in constructing a Linked List of Nodes is exploring how one Node can reference another Node.

This code:

```
Node start = new Node(10, null);
```

allocates a Node object, setting its *data* field to 10 and its *next* field to **null**. Figure 30 shows this, introducing a new graphic representation for a reference variable and its referent. The reference variable *start* is shown as a box, with its name located just above. The Node object referred to, or pointed to, is shown as a box containing the *data* field contents, 10, and for its *next* field, an 'electrical ground' symbol representing a null object reference. If *next* referenced another Node, it would have an arrow symbol pointing to that Node.

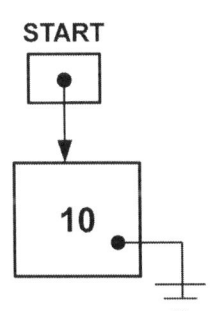

Figure 30: start References Node Containing '10'

Suppose that the following three lines of code are executed:

```
(1)    Node start = new Node(10, null);
(2)    start = new Node(15, start);
(3)    start = new Node(20, start);
```

As discussed above, Line 1 gives the result in Figure 30. When Line 2 executes, remember that the expression on the right hand side of the '=' sign is fully evaluated first, before the assignment into the left hand side variable, *start*, takes place. That means that when the Node having its *value* set to '15' is created, it also has its *next* field set to the **same reference that *start* is pointing to**, which is the Node containing *value* '10'. After the '15' Node is initialized, the last step of Line 2 is to change *start* so that it now references the newly created, Figure 31 shows the configuration after line 2 has executed.

The same process is repeated in Line 3, creating a new Node with *value* '20', and *next* set to point to the '15' Node, finally moving *start* to point to this new Node. See Figure 32.

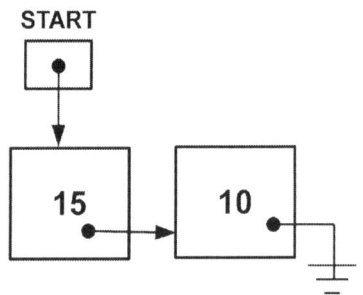

Figure 31: start *References Node Containing '15', Which References Node Containing '10'*

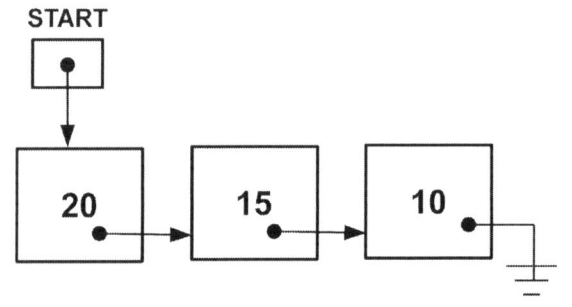

Figure 32: start *References Node '20', the Beginning of the Linked List of Nodes*

It is obvious that this 'hard-coded', in-variable sequence of lines of code used to create this linked list is unwieldy, and not suited for building larger lists. Instead, it would be convenient to *abstract* this structure into an ADT, and then build a Java class which will implement it.

THE DYNAMIC LINKED LIST

Advantages and Disadvantages of the Linked List structure

The Linked List concept has several advantages over the static array structures discussed in previous chapters. First, Linked Lists are completely dynamic, and require virtually no space to be allocated for an empty list, and can be enlarged to any size, limited only by the memory available to the program. A static array must be allocated as some initial size at run time, and resizing it is computationally expensive, requiring the movement of all its elements to a new memory allocation. Second, Linked Lists are flexible, and the insertion or deletion of elements does not require the movement of data in order to prevent gaps in the structure. Arrays, on the other hand, require data to be moved in order to maintain a contiguous sequence of values, or alternatively, some management scheme to keep track of, or search for, vacant locations which are available for use.

The major disadvantage of the Linked List is the lack of indexed, or 'random' access to the data elements. To find the fourth element in a linked list, one must traverse– that is, *travel past*– the first, second, and third elements, because there is no way to go directly to an element. In contrast, an array allows any element to be accessed efficiently by its index number, allowing for the application of effective algorithms such as the *Binary Search,* which relies upon the ability to efficiently find the middle value in the search space. In an application where fast indexed access is required, the array generally provides a more effective structure than the Linked List.

Chapter Checklist

- ❏ Linked Lists provide a flexible data structure which allocates and deallocates space as needed at runtime, and never needs to use more space than is actually needed.

- ❏ A Linked List can be built using a simple Node class as the basic list element. Such a Node has fields to store the necessary data, and a 'next 'Node' reference variable (*often named* next *for convenience*) to link to its successor Node in the list.

- ❏ All object reference variables in Java are the same size, so the compiler is able to allow for self-referencing class definitions, such as is seen in the Node class.

- ❏ Advantages of the Linked List over a static array are 1) its totally flexible size which can be modified while the program is running, with no wasted space, and 2) the ability to insert and remove elements anywhere in the list without the need to physically move any data in memory.

- ❏ The major disadvantage of the Linked List when compared to an array is the lack of indexed, direct access to an element, requiring the traversal of all the preceding elements in order to reach the desired element.

> **I can't change the direction of the wind,
> but I can adjust my sails to always
> reach my destination.**
> *– Jimmy Dean*

Chapter 14: The Double-Ended List ADT

The Double Ended List ADT is a data structure in which multiple values can be stored. It is commonly implemented using the concept of the Dynamic Linked List, but it could actually be implemented with an Array as its underlying storage structure. The main justification for using a Linked List implementation is that space can be allocated and deallocated as needed at program runtime. The List described here:
    1) has no indexing,
    2) is pictured as a sequence of values oriented horizontally, left to right,
    3) allows values to be added at or removed from either its left- or its right-end,
    4) provides no access to any interior values,
    5) maintains the sequence in which the values were
       added to the list.

The interface for this List ADT is described in detail below.

The Double-Ended List Interface

The List developed here is an abstract data structure which is defined entirely apart from the manner in which it is implemented. As with the ADTs previously discussed, Double-Ended List ADT is defined by the interface which it presents to the world:

*The integer version of the Double-Ended List ADT is used to manage a list of integer items (type **int**), and operates in the following manner. The list may be pictured as a series of integer values ordered from left to right. New values may be added to the left end of the list using the InsertLeft method, or added to the right end of the list using the InsertRight method. Similarly, values are removed from the list using the RemoveLeft or RemoveRight methods. The isEmpty method returns true if there are no values in the list. Care should be taken to test whether the list is empty before attempting the RemoveLeft or RemoveRight operations. If the list is empty and a removal is attempted, the error value specified when the list was constructed is returned. The specific method signatures are:*

> **LinkedList(int errorValue)** – *This constructor accepts errorValue as the value to be returned if a remove operation is attempted on an empty list.*
>
> **boolean isEmpty()** – *returns **true** if the list is empty.*
>
> **void InsertLeft(int data)** – *adds data to left end of the list.*
>
> **int RemoveLeft()** – *removes and returns the leftmost value from the list. If the list is empty, returns the errorValue specified in the ADT constructor.*
>
> **void InsertRight(int data)** – *adds data to right end of the list.*
>
> **int RemoveRight()** – *removes and returns the rightmost value from the list. If the list is empty, returns the errorValue specified in the constructor.*

THE DOUBLE-ENDED LIST ADT

int Size() – *returns the number of elements in the list.*

void Display() – *displays the list values, one per line, to the standard output.*

Given this interface description, a programmer can understand the correct use of the Linked List ADT, even though there is no description of exactly *how* the list is implemented in code. Such details are not necessary in order to use the data structure, and, in fact, would be distracting to any programmers who simply want to use this ADT in their project.

It should be noted that, for illustrative purposes, only the integer version of the List ADT is described above. However, this ADT is completely adaptable to the storage of any other kind of data element, including class types, by substituting that type name wherever int appears in the interface.

The following code segment gives an example of a main program which utilizes the List ADT, as implemented by a class called LinkedList, which will be described shortly:

```
1  // main program to test the List ADT
2
3
4  public class Main {
5
6  public static void main(String[] args) {
7     // declare the list, error flag is -99
8     LinkedList mylist = new LinkedList(-99);
9     // listValue accepts removed data
10    int listValue;
11
12    // add six items to the list
13    mylist.InsertLeft(10);
14    mylist.InsertLeft(9);
15    mylist.InsertLeft(8);
16    mylist.InsertRight(7);
```

```java
17     mylist.InsertRight(6);
18     mylist.InsertRight(5);
19
20     // show the list as it is now
21     System.out.println("The list now contains "+
22             mylist.Size()+" nodes.");
23     mylist.Display();
24
25     // example of safely removing from the list
26     if (mylist.isEmpty() == false){
27         listValue = mylist.RemoveLeft();
28         System.out.println("Removed "+listValue+
29             " from the left end.");
30     }
31
32     mylist.Display();
33
34     // as long as the list is not empty, remove
35     while (!mylist.isEmpty()){
36         listValue = mylist.RemoveRight();
37         System.out.println("Removed "+listValue+
38             " from the right end.");
39         mylist.Display();
40         System.out.println();
41     }
42
43     System.out.println("The list now contains "+
44             mylist.Size()+" nodes.");
45
```

```
46      // finally, show value returned when
47      //   try to remove from empty list
48      listValue = mylist.RemoveRight();
49      System.out.println("After list was empty,"
                +listValue+
50              " returned from RemoveRight.");
51    }
52 }
```

The above code is intended to be self-explanatory, as it simply creates a list object, adds data to it, and then removes the data values, finally emptying the list. It should be compared to the output from the run of this program as listed below.

```
run:
The list now contains 6 nodes.
List contents:
  8
  9
  10
  7
  6
  5
------------------
Removed 8 from the left end.
List contents:
  9
  10
  7
  6
  5
------------------
Removed 5 from the right end.
List contents:
  9
  10
  7
```

```
  6
------------------

Removed 6 from the right end.
List contents:
  9
  10
  7
------------------

Removed 7 from the right end.
List contents:
  9
  10
------------------

Removed 10 from the right end.
List contents:
  9
------------------

Removed 9 from the right end.
List contents:
------------------

The list now contains 0 nodes.
After list was empty, -99 returned from RemoveRight.
BUILD SUCCESSFUL (total time: 0 seconds)
```

Implementing the Double-Ended List ADT as a Linked List

Now that the interface for the List ADT has been defined, the next step is understanding the details of implementing this data structure as a *linked list* of nodes. There will actually be two different Java classes involved in implementing the linked list.

THE DOUBLE-ENDED LIST ADT

The Node Class

The first class to be considered for this implementation is the Node class, a slight variation of the Node class presented in detail in the previous chapter. The functioning is identical, though here, the constructor parameters are named differently:

```
 1
 2
 3 public class Node {
 4     int value;
 5     Node next;
 6
 7     public Node(int newData, Node nextRef){
 8         value = newData;
 9         next = nextRef;
10     }
11 }
```

The Linked List Class

The dynamic version of the Double-Ended List ADT will create a sequence of Node objects where each one points to the next Node in the sequence through its *next* data field. The Linked List only needs to keep track of the first Node in the list (considered here to be the 'leftmost' Node) . The first Node will refer to the second, the second refers to the third, and so on, forming a chain of connected Nodes. The last Node in the list will have its *next* field set to null to indicate that it is at the end of the list (which is considered, here, to be the 'rightmost' Node).

The LinkedList class code listing below shows how the List can be implemented. There is a detailed explanation included for each method.

```
 1
 2
 3  public class LinkedList {
 4      private Node start;   //refers to left end
 5      private int errorReturn;
 6
```

First, the data fields defined are the left end of the list, *start*, and the value to be returned when a removal is attempted on an empty list, *errorReturn*. These are the only needed data elements (lines 4-5).

```
 7      // constructor accepts value to be returned
 8      // if a Remove is called on empty list
 9      public LinkedList(int errorValue) {
10          start = null;
11          errorReturn = errorValue;
12      }
13
```

The constructor will ensure that *start* is set to null when the list is created, and also store the value to be returned on a Remove error (7-12).

```
14      // returns true if list has no elements
15      public boolean isEmpty(){
16          return (start == null);
17      }
18
```

isEmpty() simply checks whether *start* is null to determine if the list is currently empty (14-17).

THE DOUBLE-ENDED LIST ADT

```
19      // adds a new node at left (start) of list
20      public void InsertLeft(int data){
21          // start may be null
22          start = new Node(data, start);
23      }
24
```

InsertLeft() creates a new Node, setting its *value* to the *data* passed in, and sets the new Node's *next* reference to *start* (19-23). *(Note that this code in Line 22 is identical to the list building code expounded in the previous Linked List chapter.)* When done, *start* will be pointing to the newly created Node, and the new Node will point to the old Node to which *start* was referring. If *start* was null, this still works, as the new Node will simply point to null, indicating the end of the list.

Figure 34 illustrates the result of adding a Node to the left end of the list shown in Figure 33, by a call to *InsertLeft(20)*. The new Node with the value '20' is created with its *next* field referencing the Node containing '15', and the list *start* variable is updated to point to the new Node.

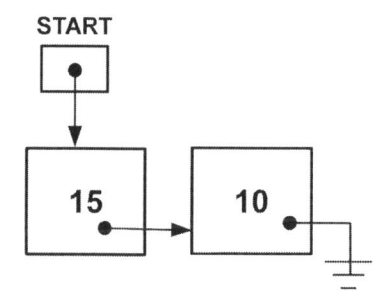

Figure 33: Existing linked list of two nodes prior to calling InsertLeft(20)

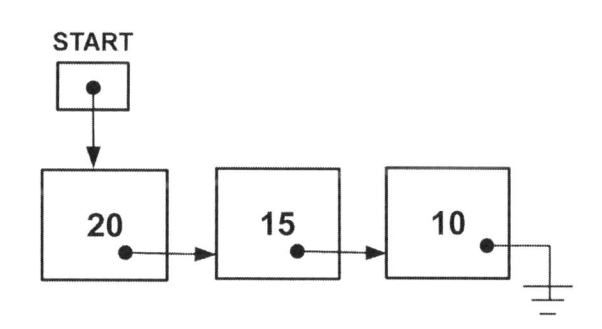

Figure 34: Expanded linked list of three nodes following call InsertLeft(20)

```
25      // removes node referred to by start;  if
26      // empty list, returns error value
27      public int RemoveLeft() {
28        int returnVal;
29        if (isEmpty())  // no good value to return
30          returnVal = errorReturn;
31        else
32          {
33            returnVal = start.value;   //save data value
34            start = start.next;        //move start over
35          }
36        return returnVal;
37      }
38
```

RemoveLeft() temporarily stores the data value contained in the *value* field of the leftmost Node (the one pointed to by *start*) in *returnVal* if the list is not empty. If the list is empty, the return value is set to the stored *errorReturn* value, otherwise the list *start* variable is changed to point to the second Node in the list (27-37). The previous first Node is no longer referenced by any variable, and becomes unreachable from the program. It will be *garbage collected* as previously discussed, and its space will be made available for future object allocation. Again, Figure 33 and 34 can be used to illustrate the process, with Figure 34 showing the List before calling *RemoveLeft()*, and Figure 33 showing the result.

The *InsertRight()* method is somewhat more complicated that its left-end counterpart. This is because of the decision to use a single *start* variable to point to the beginning of the List. In order to find the right end of the List, the method will begin checking at the *start*-referenced Node, then step through the remainder of the List until the Node having a **null** *next* field is found. This is done using the variable *curNode*, as shown below:

THE DOUBLE-ENDED LIST ADT

```
39      // adds a new node at 'right' end of list
40      public void InsertRight(int data){
41          Node currNode;   //used to move through list
42          // if start is null, just create new Node
43          if (start == null)
44            start = new Node(data, start);
45          else
46          // start points to something, so look for end
47           {
48             currNode = start; //begin at left end
49             // the last node has next == null
50             while (currNode.next != null){
51                 currNode = currNode.next;
52             }
53             // currnode is where new node is to be added
54             currNode.next = new Node(data, null);
55           }
56      }
57
```

InsertRight() (39-56) adds a new node to the right end of the list. If *start* is null, a 1-Node list is created (43-44), as was done in *InsertLeft()*. Otherwise, a Node reference variable called *currNode* is used to move through the list from left to right, beginning at *start*, until it refers to the final Node, which currently has its *next* field set to null (50-51). The initial setting of *curNode* is shown in Figure 35, where both *start* and *curNode* are referencing the '20' Node.

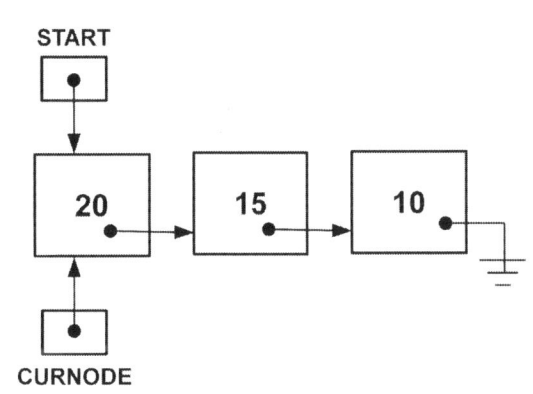

Figure 35: *In* InsertRight(5) *call, position of* curNode *when the search for the last Node begins*

Updating *currNode* in the line:

```
51 currNode = currNode.next;
```

illustrates a very common and important linked-list programming technique for moving through a list. This, in effect, moves *currNode* 'ahead', so that it refers to each of the nodes in the list, in sequence, until the ending condition of the while loop in line 50 becomes **true**. Understanding this simple idea is essential to working with dynamically linked structures of any kind.

Figure 36 shows the movement of *curNode* inside of the **while** loop at Line 50, and Figure 37 shows *curNode* when the **while** loop terminates due to *curNode.next* being equal to **null**. At this point, the last Node in the list has been located, and at Line 54, *curNode.next* is updated to point to the new Node, as shown in Figure 38.

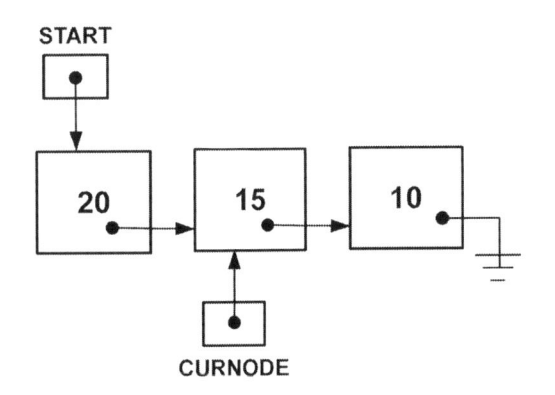

Figure 36: *In* InsertRight(5) *call, position of* curNode *while seeking the last Node*

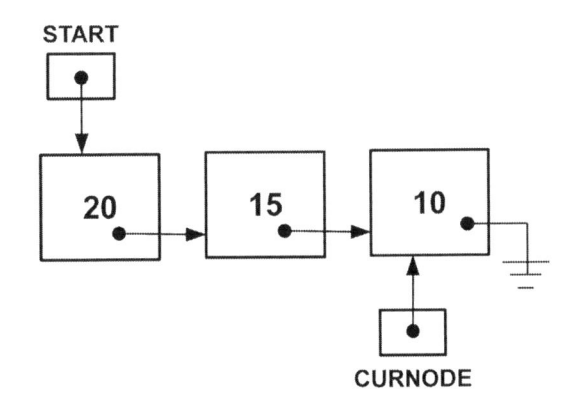

Figure 37: *In* InsertRight(5) *call, position of* curNode *with the last Node found*

THE DOUBLE-ENDED LIST ADT

The *RemoveRight()* implementation uses a similar process of moving through the entire list to find the last node, but in this case, it is not the final Node, but the next-to-last Node which that must be found in order to delete the last Node. This is accomplished by introducing the concept of moving two Node pointers simultaneously through the List: a *currNode*, which leads the search through the list, and a *prevNode* variable, which follows behind, moving in parallel with *currNode*. Figure 39 shows the initial assignment of *currNode* and *prevNode* before the **while** loop begins executing. By setting *prevNode* to **null** initially, it is possible to recognize the special case of a List containing just one Node, which must be handled differently from the multiple-Node List.

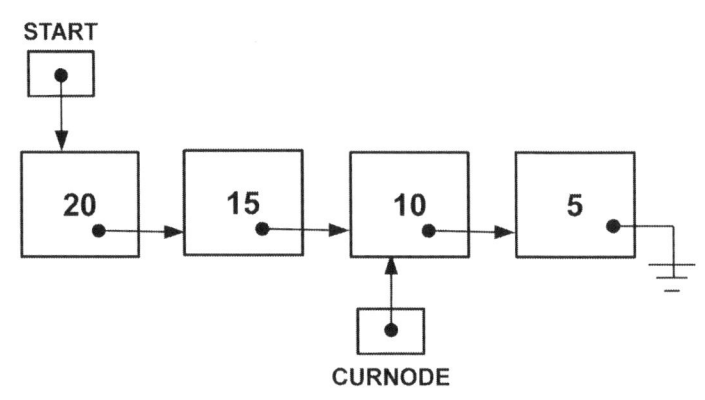

Figure 38: *In* InsertRight(5) *call, final creation of '5' Node, referenced by* curNode.next

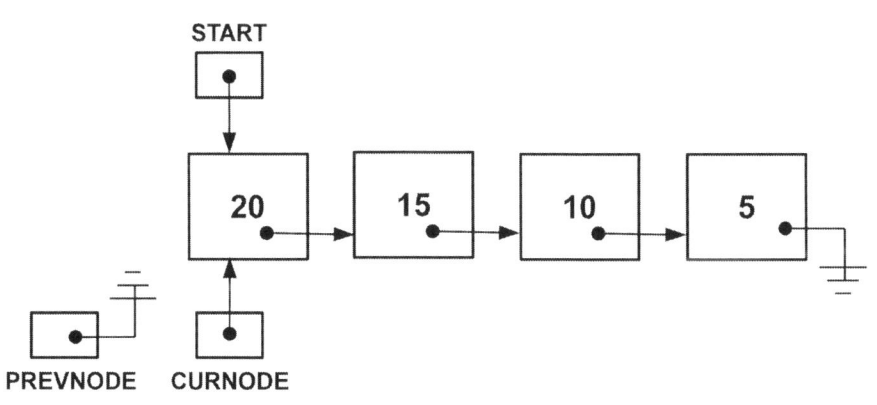

Figure 39: *Initial arrangement of* prevNode *and* curNode *when* RemoveRight() *is called.*

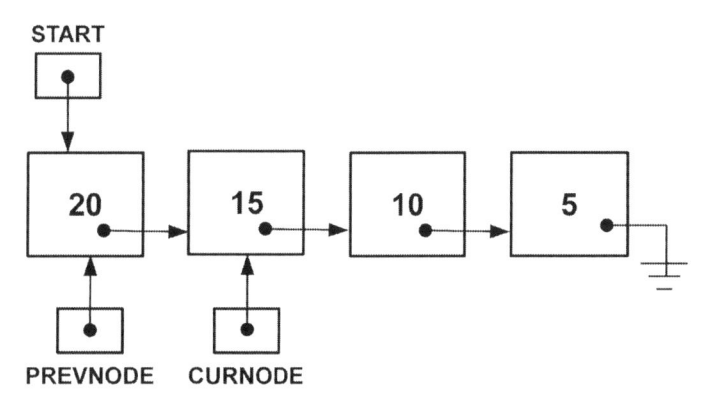

Figure 40: prevNode *and* curNode *updated after first* **while** *loop iteration in* RemoveRight() *call.*

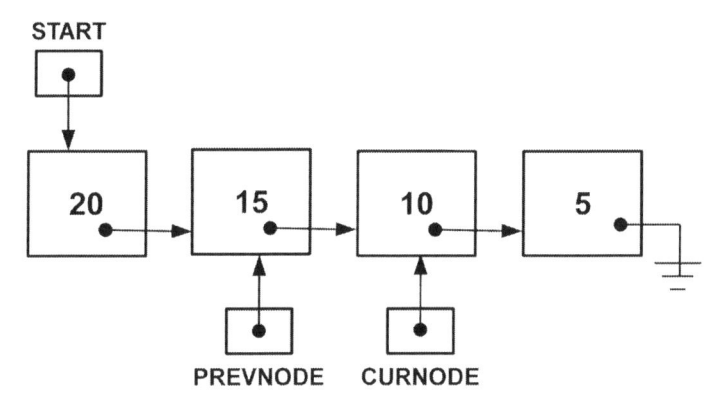

Figure 41: prevNode *and* curNode *updated after second* **while** *loop iteration in* RemoveRight() *call.*

THE DOUBLE-ENDED LIST ADT

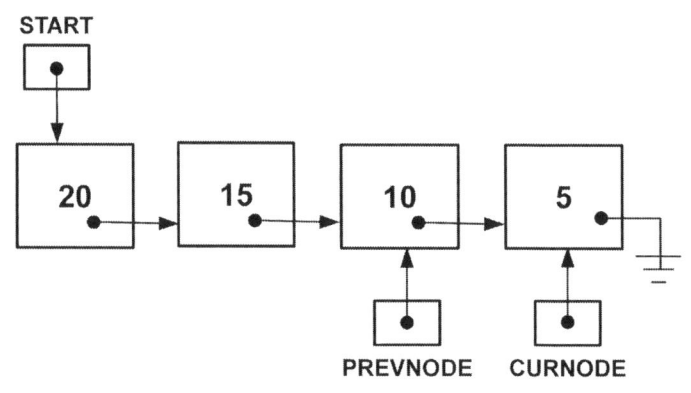

Figure 42: prevNode *and* curNode *updated after third* **while** *loop iteration in* RemoveRight() *call.* curNode.next *is* **null**, *and* prevNode.next *will be set to* **null** *to delete the Node with value '5'*

RemoveRight() returns the value contained in the rightmost Node after it removes the Node from the list. If the list is empty (64-65), *returnVal* is assigned the preset *errorReturn* value, otherwise it will be set to the value stored in the last Node in the list, once it is found. Lines 68-75 move two reference pointers through the list, as shown in Figures 40, 41, and 42. This is a common and important technique. *currNode* is used to find the last Node in the list by moving through the list and looking for the Node having a null *next* field. *prevNode* is assigned the value of *currNode* just before *currNode* is updated, so that *prevNode* points to the node behind *currNode*. This way, the value to be returned from the last node can be assigned into *returnVal* (77), and the next-to-last Node, pointed to by *prevNode*, can have its *next* field set to null, deleting the last Node from the list (82-83).

```java
58      // removes 'right' end node
59      // if empty list, returns error value
60      public int RemoveRight() {
61         int returnVal;
62         Node currNode, prevNode;    //list place holders
63
64         if (isEmpty())   // no good value to return
65            returnVal = errorReturn;
66         else
67          {
68          // find the last and next-to-last nodes
69          currNode = start; //begin at left end
70          prevNode = null; //maybe only 1 node in list!
71          // the last node has next == null
72          while (currNode.next != null){
73              prevNode = currNode;       //save this spot
74              currNode = currNode.next; //advance through
75              }
76          // currnode is node to delete
77          returnVal = currNode.value;  //save data value
78          // prevNode never moved if just 1 node in list
79          if (prevNode == null)  // never changed
80            start = null;
81          else
82          // prevNode refers to currNode, delete currNode
83             prevNode.next = null; // new end of the list
84          }
85        return returnVal;
86      }
87
```

In order to handle the situation where there was only one Node left in the list when *RemoveRight()* was called, it is necessary to check whether *prevNode* has been updated from its initial null value (78-79). If there was a single Node in the list, the **while** loop at (72-75) would not have been entered at all, and *prevNode* will still be null. Therefore, in order to remove the only Node left, *start* must be set to null (80).

THE DOUBLE-ENDED LIST ADT

The method *Size()* (listing below) counts through the list to determine how many Nodes are present. First, it initializes the *length* variable, which it will finally return, to zero (90). A *currNode* reference is set to *start*, the beginning of the list. Each iteration of the while loop (93-96) increments *length* and moves *currNode* ahead in the list. Notice that, if the list is empty, *currNode* will initially be set to null, the while loop will never be entered, and length will remain at zero.

```
88          // Return the current length of list
89          public int Size() {
90              int length = 0;            // number of nodes
91              Node currNode = start;    // list position
92              // move through list, counting nodes
93              while (currNode != null) {
94                  length++;
95                  currNode = currNode.next;
96              }
97              return length;
98          }
99
```

In order to complete the *LinkedList* capabilities, a *Display()* method is included so that the list contents can be easily displayed.

```
100         // Display the current list contents, left to right
101         public void Display(){
102             Node currNode = start;
103             System.out.println("List contents:");
104             // step through the list
105             while (currNode != null) {
106                 System.out.println(" "+currNode.value);
107                 currNode = currNode.next;
108             }
109             System.out.println("-------------------");
110         }
111     }
```

Display() again uses the now familiar process of moving through the list with a *currNode* variable stepping to each Node. After printing a simple heading line (103), a while loop (105-108) prints the value of the Node which *currNode* points to, and moves *currNode* ahead to the next Node. An ending line is printed to complete the printout (109).

Implementing the Dynamic Stack and Queue as 'Wrapper' Classes

The following two examples show how an ADT interface can be implemented by using an existing class as the underlying storage mechanism. In this case, the Double-Ended List ADT, implemented through the *LinkedList* class, will form the storage object for both Stack and Queue implementations.

Observe, first of all, that the LinkedList can be made to act like a LIFO Stack if data items are added and removed from the same end of the list. So, a *push()* could be accomplished with an *InsertLeft()* operation, and the *pop()* would then require using a *RemoveLeft()* call. (Note that an *InsertRight()* and *RemoveRight()* pairing would have been equally usable, but less efficient due to the steps required to repeatedly traverse the list to reach the rightmost element.) The simple style of code below is often referred to as a 'wrapper' class, because it adds little or no code onto an existing class. Instead, the purpose of a 'wrapper' class is to create a different, controlled interface to the original calss. In this case, the Stack interface is wrapped around the *LinkedList* class.

```
class Stack {
 private LinkedList list;

 public Stack(){
    list = new LinkedList(-999);
 }

 public push(int x){
    list.InsertLeft(x);
 }

 public int pop(){
   return list.RemoveLeft();
 }

 public int size(){
   return list.size();
 }

 public boolean isEmpty(){
   return list.isEmpty();
 }
}
```

In a similar manner, the FIFO Queue interface can also be built around the *LinkedList* class by always adding elements at one end of the Double Ended List, and removing them from the other end. The Queue *insert()* method will be implemented using the *InsertLeft()* method, and *remove()* will utilize the *RemoveRight()* method. (The complementary methods *InsertRight()* and *RemoveLeft()* could be similarly used, and would offer equivalent efficiency of access speed in this case.) Below is the code for this simple Queue class, again implemented as a wrapper around the *LinkedList*, as was done with the Stack wrapper.

```
class Queue {
 private LinkedList list;

 public Queue(){
    list = new LinkedList(-999);
 }

 public insert(int x){
    list.InsertLeft(x);
 }

 public int remove(){
   return list.RemoveRight();
 }

 public int size(){
   return list.size();
 }
 public boolean isEmpty(){
   return list.isEmpty();
 }
}
```

Applying the Wrapper Class Concept

These two wrapper class examples show how easy it is to implement an ADT by building its interface around an underlying storage class. The interface presented to the ADT user contains exactly the method calls and behavior expected, while the reality of the actual implementation is completely hidden. In fact, two completely different interfaces, that of the *Stack* and that of the *Queue,* can be built around the same *LinkedList* class.

Software engineering efforts apply this type of interface development to construct a desired interface very rapidly by building upon the foundation of an existing ADT component. This allows high-level proof-of-concept tests to be created quickly with a minimal amount of effort. By creating models using ADTs, the design process of new or exploratory software is facilitated by using concept-level structures, while avoiding implementation details.

The downside of building wrapper classes is that a degree of computational overhead is added to every process. Instead of a single, direct call to a method, the wrapper method is called, which then calls the underlying method. Because such wrapping is not limited, it is possible to construct multiple levels of wrapping, and greatly multiply the number of method calls taking place. The computational cost of a method call is negligible when considered on a one-at-a-time basis– a matter of micro- or mili-seconds. But when millions of method calls are made in a high-performance, time-critical application, the overhead of wrappers can become prohibitive for the final program. But, when used in less-demanding situations, the wrapper class concept can be a useful, low-effort means of constructing a well-designed, easy to implement ADT interface for either proto-typing or for final product use.

Chapter Checklist

❏ The Double-Ended List ADT is a structure which allows access to data through adding or deleting items on either the left or right end of the list. Values are maintained in the sequence in which they were added to the list.

❏ The Double-Ended List interface includes the method calls: *isEmpty()*, *InsertLeft()*, *RemoveLeft()*, *InsertRight()*, *RemoveRight()*, *Size()*, and *Display()*.

❏ The pointer management techniques used to implement the Double-Ended List should be studied and understood, because they are commonly used, and useful to master.

❏ A *wrapper class* is one which constructs an interface around another class, using some subset of the methods of the original class as needed to obtain the desired behavior. This approach can facilitate rapid prototyping and testing of design options. Wrapper classes impose a slight performance overhead which may be unacceptable in some high-performance portions of a final program product.

> The five essential entrepreneurial skills
> for success are concentration,
> discrimination, organization, innovation
> and communication.
> – *Michael Faraday, physicist*

Chapter 15: The Dynamic Stack and Queue

As discussed in the previous chapter, it is possible to use the Double-Ended List as the storage mechanism for implementing a dynamic version of either the Stack or the Queue ADT. This chapter illustrates the direct implementation of these ADTs, showing how simply the two can be built using the basic linked list concepts.

Revisiting the *Node* Class

The *Node* class described previously is used for the Stack and Queue. Each *Node* contains an **int** named *data*, and a **Node** reference named *next*.

```
1 public class Node {
2       int data;
3       Node next;
4
5       Node(int value, Node nxt){
6           data = value;
7           next = nxt;
8       }
9 }
```

The constructor is designed to allow both the *data* and *next* fields to be initialized when the Node is created.

Implementing the *Stack*
The *Stack* interface is the same as previously described: *push()*, *pop()*, *isEmpty*, and *size()*. The code is listed below, with commentary.

```
1 package linkedstackqueue;
2
3 public class Stack {
4     private Node top;
5     private int numelements;
```

The *Stack* class data fields are the **Node** reference *top*, and an **int** *numelements* counter which keeps track of the number of Nodes which have been created.

```
6      //Constructor
7      public Stack(){
8          top = null;
9          numelements = 0;
10     }
```

The *Stack* class constructor initializes the data to an empty *Stack*.

```
11      //push() adds at top of list
12      public void push(int val){
13          top = new Node(val, top);
14          //increment element counter
15          numelements++;
16      }
```

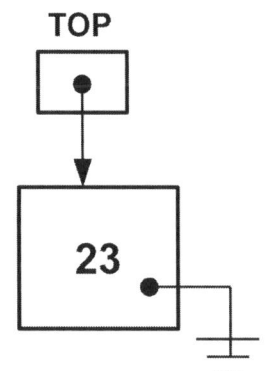

TOP

The *push* method creates a new *Node* containing the pushed **int** *val* and referencing the previous top *Node*. The *top* variable references the newly created *Node*. Figure 43 shows the result of calling *push(23)*, with *top* referencing the *Node*. *numelements* is updated to reflect an additional stack entry. Figure 44 shows the result following a call to *push(18)*, with the new *Node* referencing the old top *Node*.

Figure 43: Stack after push(23) call

```
17      //pop() removes and returns top element
18      public int pop(){
19          //save return value
20          int temp = top.data;
21          //move top 'down' the list
22          top = top.next;
23          //decrement element counter
24          numelements--;
25          return temp;
26      }
```

pop() returns the value contained in the topmost *Node*, advancing *top* so that it references the next *Node* down in the *Stack*. *numelements* is decremented to indicate the decrease in the *Stack* size. Figures 43 and 44, in reverse order, show the result of a *pop()* operation.

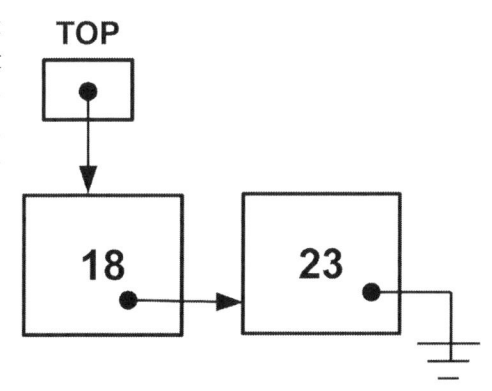

Figure 44: *Stack after push(18) call*

```
27      //size of list using counter
28      public int size1(){
29           return numelements;
30      }
```

Two versions of *size()* are implemented here. The simple one, *size1()*, simply returns the *numelements* counter.

THE DYNAMIC STACK AND QUEUE

```
31      //size of list by traversing list
32      public int size2(){
33          Node current;
34          //start at top element
35          current = top;
36          int count = 0;
37          //look for the end of the list
38          while (current != null)
39          {
40             count++;
41             current = current.next;
42          }
43          return count;
44      }
```

The *size2()* method is included to show a way to count the *Nodes* in the *Stack* by starting a reference at the *top Node*, and stepping through the list, incrementing the count for each *Node* encountered, until the *current* reference reaches the end of the list and becomes **null**.

```
45      //isEmpty checks top
46      public boolean isEmpty(){
47          return (top==null);
48      }
```

The *isEmpty()* condition is **true** if top has been set to **null**. Finally, the *display()* method, below, prints the *Stack* by moving the *curr* reference through the list, printing each *Node* value as it is encountered. The typical output looks like:

```
TOP- | 10 | 5 | 12 | 8 | -BOTTOM
```

```
49      //display() prints current stack contents
50      public void display(){
51          //start at top of list
52          Node curr = top;
53          System.out.print("TOP- | ");
54          //Look for end of list, printing each data value
55          while (curr != null){
56              System.out.print(curr.data+" | ");
57              curr = curr.next;
58          }
59        System.out.println("-BOTTOM");
60      }
61      }
62 }
```

Implementing the *Queue*

The *Queue* interface is the same as previously described: *insert()*, *remove()*, *isEmpty*, and *size()*. The code follows.

```
1 package linkedstackqueue;
2 public class Queue {
3     private Node front, rear;
4     //Constructor
5     public Queue(){
6         front = null;
7         rear = null;
8     }
```

The *Queue* utilizes two *Node* references, *front* and *rear*. The constructor sets both of these to **null**. Elements are added to the *next* field of the *Node* referenced by *rear*, and removed by removing the *Node* referenced by *front*.

THE DYNAMIC STACK AND QUEUE

```
 9      //Queue inserts new values at rear
10      public void insert(int val){
11          //If empty list, create 1 Node, with
12          // front and rear both referencing it
13          if (front==null){
14              front = new Node(val,null);
15              rear = front;
16          }
17          //Adding to existing list
18          else {
19              //Append new Node at rear
20              rear.next = new Node(val,null);
21              //Update rear to reference the end
22              rear = rear.next;
23          }
24      }
```

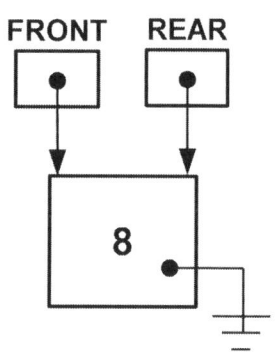

Figure 45: *Queue after insert(8) call*

The *insert()* method must check for the special case of an empty *Queue*. For an empty list, a new *Node* is created, and both *front* and *rear* are set to reference the same *Node* (lines 11-17). Otherwise, the *next* field of the *rear Node* is assigned to reference the newly created *Node*, and then *rear* is updated to point to that new *Node* (lines 19-22). Figure 45 shows the configuration of a newly created *Queue* following the call *insert(8)*, with *front* and *rear* both referencing the *Node* containing the value 8. Figure 46 shows what happens if *insert(11)* is then called, leaving *front* still referencing the '8' *Node*, and *rear* now pointing to the '11' *Node*. Following *insert(24)*, the *Queue* will be in the configuration shown in Figure 47.

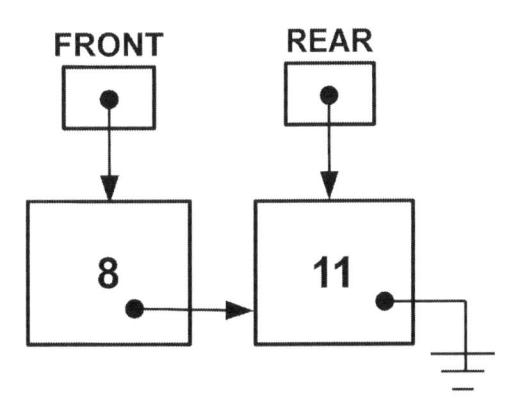

Figure 46: *Queue after insert(11) call*

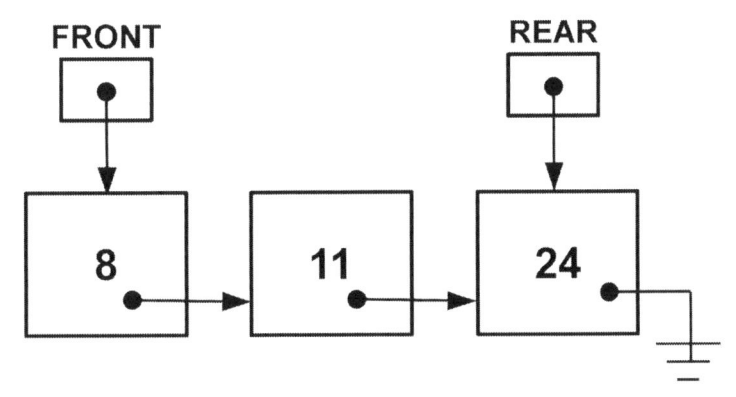

Figure 47: *Queue after insert(24) call*

THE DYNAMIC STACK AND QUEUE

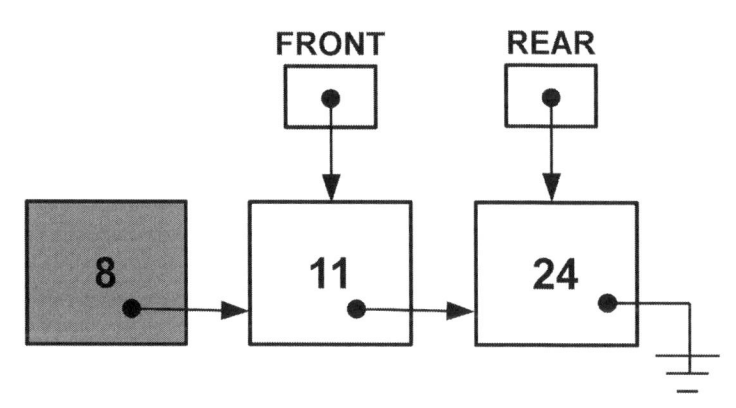

Figure 48: Queue after remove() has been called. Node '8' will be deallocated from memory.

```
25      //Queue removes from front of list
26      public int remove(){
27          //store the return value
28          int temp = front.data;
29          //Move front toward rear
30          front = front.next;
31          return temp;
32      }
```

The *remove()* method saves the *data* value referenced by *front*, which is to be returned, then moves *front* to the next *Node* in the *Queue*. Figure 48 shows the result of calling *remove()* on the *Queue* as shown in the previous Figure 47. *front* has been advanced to reference the '11' *Node*, and the '8' *Node* is greyed out to indicate that it has been deleted from the *Queue*, and its allocated space will ultimately be reclaimed during the 'garbage-collection' activity of the Java Virtual Machine.

```
33      //isEmpty() checks front
34      public boolean isEmpty(){
35          return (front==null);
36      }
```

-173-

isEmpty() simply returns **true** if *front* is set to **null**.

```
37      //Count number of Nodes in list
38      public int size(){
39          //Start at front of list
40          int count = 0;
41          Node current = front;
42          //Look for other end while counting
43          while (current != null){
44              count++;
45              current = current.next;
46          }
47          return count;
48      }
```

To find the number of entries in the *Queue*, *size()* starts at *front*, and moves the reference *current* through the list, incrementing *count* for each *Node* found.

Display() uses a similar approach, but instead of counting the number of *Nodes* encountered, the values found are printed.

```
49      //display() prints the Queue contents
50      public void display(){
51          //Start at front
52          Node curr = front;
53          System.out.print("FRONT- | ");
54          //Move through list until end is found
55          while (curr != null){
56              System.out.print(curr.data+" | ");
57              curr = curr.next;
58          }
59        System.out.println("-REAR");
60      }
61  }
```

THE DYNAMIC STACK AND QUEUE

The *display()* method prints the *Queue* contents by stepping through the list and printing each data value found. The typical output looks like:

```
FRONT- | 2 | 5 | 8 | 12 | 9 | -REAR
```

Summary

Both the *Stack* and *Queue* ADTs are easily implemented as special cases of the dynamic linked list. The data type stored in each *Node* can be defined to be any Java- or user-defined type.

DESIGNING DATA STRUCTURES IN JAVA

Chapter Checklist

❏ The *Stack* ADT can be simply implemented as a dynamically linked list structure with a *top* reference variable maintained to always point to the top *Node* of the *Stack*.

❏ The key code for the *Stack push()* operation is: `top = new Node(value, top)`, creating a new object whose *next* points to the old top of the stack, and to which *top* will refer. The essential line for the *Stack pop()* is: `top = top.next` which moves the *top* pointer to the next *Node* in the *Stack*, the new top *Node*.

❏ The *Queue* ADT is only slightly more complicated than the *Stack*, maintaining both a *front* and a *rear* reference to keep track to the two ends of the *Queue*.

❏ The key code for the *insert()* method is: `rear.next = new Node(value, null)`, which adds the new *Node* to the end of the *Queue*. The important line to remember for the *remove()* method is: `front = front.next`, which moves *front* to the next available *Node* in the list.

> The trouble with organizing a thing is that pretty soon folks get to paying more attention to the organization than to what they're organized for.
> – Laura Ingalls Wilder

Chapter 16: The Dynamic Ordered List

As the final discussion of the linked list as a linear structure, this chapter revisits the *OrderedList* ADT previously implemented using an array for storage. This dynamic linked list implementation has two advantages over the array version: 1) space is only allocated as needed to accommodate the actual size of the list, and 2) data never has to be moved to open a new slot or to remove a gap after deletion. These advantages will be explained in describing the actual code being used.

Recapping the OrderedList ADT Interface

The interface being implemented here is the same as that which was implemented using the array storage, with slight adaptation as appropriate to the removal of space limitations in this dynamic version. Briefly:

    void Add(int value) – *adds* value *to the list in ascending sorted order, and cannot fail.*

    boolean Remove(int value) – *returns* false *only if* value *was not found in the list, otherwise removes* value *and returns* true.

int Size() *– returns the current number of items contained in the list.*

boolean Find(int value) *– returns* **true** *if* value *is in the list.*

void Display() *– prints out the current contents of the list (there are no indices).*

The implementation of each of these methods is described below:

```
1
2
3  public class OrderedList {
4      private Node start;   //refers to left end of list
5
6      public OrderedList() {
7          start = null;
8      }
```

The *OrderedList* class needs only the single *start* reference to maintain the list.

The *Add()* method searches for the first value in the list which is **greater than** the value *x* which is being added. It must handle, first, the special case of adding a value to an empty list. Here, it just creates a new *Node* for *start* to reference. The second special case is when the new value is to be added at the front of the list, ahead of the value pointed to by *start*. This requires *start* to point to the new *Node,* and the new *Node* to point to what *was* the first *Node*. Beyond these situations, the variable *curr* is moved through the list, checking first to see if it has come to the end of the list (lines 24-27), and then to see if *curr.next.value* is greater than *x* (lines 30-32).

THE DYNAMIC ORDERED LIST

```
 9    //Adds x value in sorted order
10    public void Add(int x){
11       boolean done = false;
12       Node curr;
13       //if list is empty, just make new one
14       if (start==null)
15          start = new Node(x,null);
16       else
17          //check if new node goes in front
18          if (start.value > x)
19             start = new Node(x,start);
20          else
21           {curr = start;
22            while (!done){
23               //if at end of list, add new node-- done
24               if (curr.next == null){
25                  curr.next = new Node(x,null);
26                  done = true;
27               }
28               else
29                  //if found x < next node, add between
30                  if (curr.next.value > x){
31                     curr.next = new Node(x,curr.next);
32                     done = true;
33                  }
34                  else
35                     //move ahead, keep looking
36                     curr = curr.next;
37            }
38
39         }
40      }
```

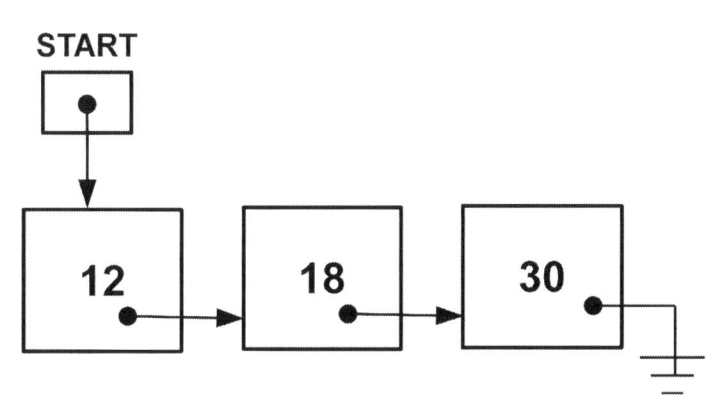

Figure 49 depicts an *OrderedList* containing three *Nodes*. The result of a call to *Add(22)* is shown in Figure 50. Here, *curr* was advanced to point to the '18' *Node,* and stopped there because *curr.next.value* contained the value '30', which is greater than the value being added, '22'. The new *Node* was created, containing the value '22', and with its *next* field pointing to *curr.next*. *Curr.next* was then set to reference the new *Node*.

Figure 49: *OrderedList with three Nodes in sequence*

A major advantage of this method of implementing the *OrderedList* over the array version is that there is no need to move all of the higher-valued entries in ordered to make space for the new entry. In the array implementation, it was necessary to move data to open a location for the new value, so that the data could be kept contiguous, with no intervening gaps between the data. However, since the linked list implementation has its elements ordered through reference fields, they are always sequential, with no gaps in between, at least in a *logical* sense. It makes no difference where the actual *Node* objects have been allocated in memory, because, in this abstract model, they are always 'next to' each other within the list, regardless of their physical locations. This can greatly improve performance when dealing with a constantly-changing list that is being updated with insertions and deletions.

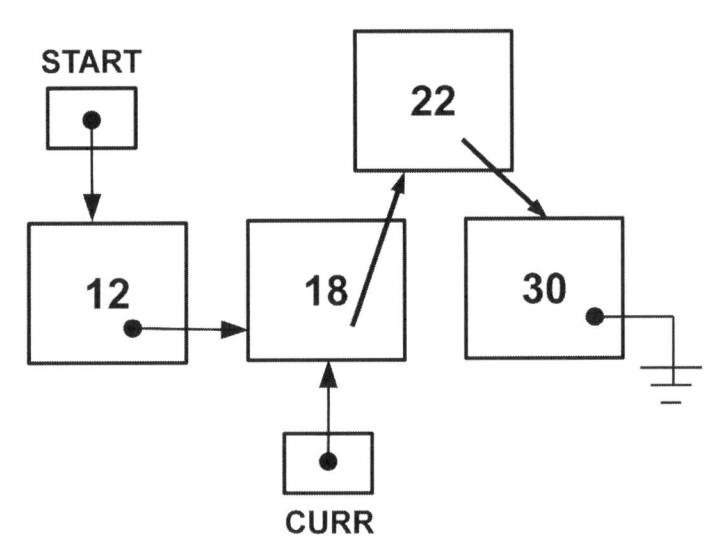

Figure 50: *OrderedList after correct placement for value '22' has been found, and the new Node has been added*

```
41      //Removes value x; if x is not in
42      // the list, returns false, otherwise true
43      public boolean Remove(int x){
44        boolean done = false;
45        boolean result = false;
46        Node curr;
47        //if list is empty, FAIL
48        if (start==null)
49          result = false;
50        else
51          //check if delete node is first, remove
52          if (start.value == x){
53            start = start.next;
54            result = true;
55          }
56          else
57            //must look further
58           {curr = start;
59            while (!done){
60              //if at end of list, cannot delete, FAIL
61              if (curr.next == null){
62                result = false;
63                done = true;
64              }
65              else
66                //if found x == next node, delete Node
67                if (curr.next.value == x){
68                  curr.next = curr.next.next;
69                  result = true;
70                  done = true;
71                }
72                else
73                  //move ahead, keep looking
74                  curr = curr.next;
75          }
76
77          }
78        return result;
79      }
```

THE DYNAMIC ORDERED LIST

The *Remove()* method is similar to the *Add()* method, in that it, too, uses a reference variable, *curr*, to move through the list in search of the value to be deleted. It handles the special cases of an empty list (lines 48-49), and the value sought being in the first node of the list, requiring *start* to be reassigned (lines 51-55). It then steps through the list, failing if it reaches the end of the list without finding the value (lines 60-64), or, if successful, re-routing the *curr.next* field around the deleted *Node* (lines 67-71). Figure 51 shows the *Node* containing '18' being deleted from the list shown in Figure 50. The variable *curr* stopped at *Node* '12', because *curr.next.value* was equal to the sought-after value, '18'. Then, *curr.next* was re-routed to point past the '18' *Node*, and instead point to *curr.next.next*, which refers to *Node* '22'. The *Node* containing '18' is greyed-out to indicate that it no longer is referenced by any variables, and will be deallocated so that its space can be reclaimed for reuse in future **new** operations.

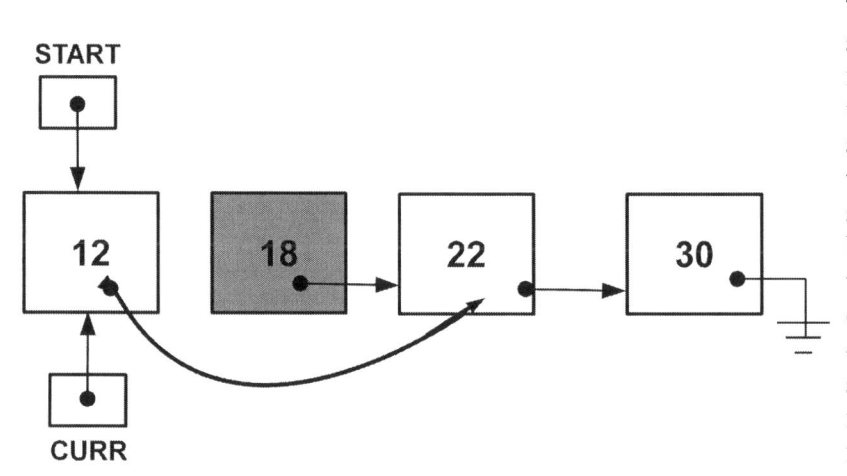

Figure 51: *OrderedList after* Remove(18) *call, with Node '18' ready to be deallocated*

The *Size()* method uses the established means of counting *Nodes* by walking through the list beginning at *start*, and continuing until the **null** reference is encountered.

```
80      // Return the current length of list
81      public int Size() {
82          int length = 0;         // number of nodes
83          Node currNode = start;  // list position
84          // move through list, counting nodes
85          while (currNode != null) {
86              length++;
87              currNode = currNode.next;
88          }
89          return length;
90      }
```

Find() similarly moves through the list, seeking the value *x*, stopping either when the value is located, or when the end of the list is reached.

```
91
92      public boolean Find(int x){
93        Node curr;
94        boolean found = false;
95        if (start != null){
96          curr = start;
97          while ((!found)&&(curr != null)){
98            found = (curr.value == x);
99            if (!found)
100              curr = curr.next;
101         }
102       }
103       return found;
104     }
```

Finally, *Display()* prints each *Node* value, moving through the list to visit each one.

```
105        // Display the current list contents, low to high
106        public void Display(){
107            Node currNode = start;
108            System.out.println("List contents:");
109            // step through the list
110            while (currNode != null) {
111                System.out.println(" "+currNode.value);
112                currNode = currNode.next;
113            }
114            System.out.println("-------------------");
115        }
116    }
```

Summary of the Dynamic Ordered List Implementation

The dynamic implementation of the *OrderedList* is straight-forward, and gives additional understanding of reference management when dealing with linked lists in general. By working through the algorithms which allow insertion and removal of *Nodes* from the *OrderedList*, the programmer gains the ability to develop and customize new ADT implementations using the powerful dynamic allocation techniques learned here.

Chapter Checklist

- The *OrderedList* ADT interface can be efficiently implemented using a dynamically linked list structure with a single *start* reference variable which always points to the beginning of the list.

- The key code for inserting a new Node into the list is exemplified in the update of the current Node reference with: `curr.next = new Node(value, curr.next)`

- When deleting from the list, the code to redirect the current Node reference around its *next* Node is done with: `curr.next = curr.next.next`

> The first 90 percent of the code accounts for the
> first 90 percent of the development time...
> The remaining 10 percent of the code accounts for
> the other 90 percent of the development time.
> – *Tom Cargill*

Chapter 17: Recursion

The topic of *recursion* is often a stumbling block for programmers. Some suggest that the cause of this difficulty is the 'unnatural' nature of recursive thought... hmmm... It turns out that examples of recursive thinking are common if one looks for them, though that does not make recursion less *disturbing* at times.

Consider the paradoxical statement:

THIS STATEMENT IS FALSE.

It is easy to skim superficially past the implications here. But, if the statement is false, then it is inaccurate, and its meaning must therefore be true. But, if the statement is true, then, as it states, it must be stating something false, so that it is really false... and so on, as the reasoning quickly gets into an unending cycle (the programmer's familiar **infinite loop)**, and one cannot draw a satisfactory conclusion about the validity of the statement.

Real-World Recursion

Examples of visual recursion abound. Artist M. C. Escher is closely associated with strange, recursive, and impossible images, such as the 1948 lithograph *Drawing Hands*. A quick web search will locate dozens of examples of his copyrighted work.

The interesting effect of having a picture contain an image of itself, which contains an image of itself, and so on, *ad infinitum*, is referred to as the *Droste effect*. The style was popularized by the Droste company, a Dutch cocoa manufacturer whose boxes used the image of a nurse carrying a tray holding a box with the very same image, which contained a box with the same image, *et cetera* (Figure 52). The effect has sometimes been used on book covers, showing a group of readers gathered around the same opened book, with the same cover and picture repeated endlessly in smaller and smaller versions.

Two mirrors, arranged to face each other some distance apart, with adjustment of their relative angles to each other, can produce a recursive 'infinite tunnel' effect through reflections of reflections. Another real-life recursion example occurs in audio feedback, when a microphone receives a sound, which is amplified and reproduced through a speaker, which is then picked up by the microphone, amplified, reproduced, and so on. The increasing amplification effect, left to itself, results in a high-pitched, ear-splitting sound that most listeners find extremely unpleasant.

Figure 52: Droste effect, *a picture within a picture (1904, Public Domain)*

As another example, think of yourself sitting and reading a book about someone who is sitting and reading a book about someone who is sitting and reading a book, and on and on . The idea of recursion will begin to take on some tangible meaning, even though it may not actually be a fully comfortable concept. Fortunately, the kinds of recursive problems that programmers deal with are much more concrete, and involve well-defined stopping conditions, rather than infinitely recursive situations.

A Simple Recursive Print Method

In computer science, recursion is an elegant and useful technique for solving certain kinds of problems. As an introduction, consider the simple task of printing out the sequence of consecutive integers over a given range, like *one through seven*. The obvious programming solution is to write a loop which counts from the starting value to the ending value, printing the counter each time. An example of this iterative solution, as a method, is:

```
static void printNum(int start, int end) {
    int i;
    for (i=start; i<= end; i++)
       System.out.print(i+", ");
}
```

Calling *printNum(1,7)* generates the desired output:

```
1, 2, 3, 4, 5, 6, 7,
```

But consider approaching the same problem differently, by using a *divide and conquer* perspective. *Divide and conquer* is a general methodology of breaking a larger problem into some number of smaller, easily solvable problems. The idea is, the large problem is difficult to solve all at once, but by breaking it into successive, easy problems, eventually the greater task is solved step by step.

Recursive problem solving works this way. The problem is to print a list of integers over some range. One way to solve this is to print the first integer in the range, then print the rest of the integers in the range starting one higher, using the same process, until the upper limit of the range is reached. Here is a recursive version of the *printNum()* method shown above:

```
static void printNumR(int start, int end){
    System.out.print(start+", ");
    if (start < end){
        printNumR(start+1,end);
    }
}
```

Here, the first line prints the value at the lower end of the range, *start*. If the upper end of the range has not yet been reached, *printNumR* calls itself, but with the *start* value one greater. The resulting output is exactly the same as that of the iterative *printNum()*.

By adding some additional printing statements to trace what is going on, the actual workings of the recursion are more evident. Here is the 'verbose' version, *printNumRP()*:

```
static void printNumRP(int start, int end){
  String s = "              ".substring(0,start);
  System.out.println(s+"Entering printNumR, start= "+start);
  if (start < end)
    printNumRP(start+1,end);
  else
    System.out.println(s+"End of the recursion!");
  System.out.println(s+"Exiting printNumR, start = "+start);
}
```

The string *s* is used to change the indent of each call, as it is initialized to contain *start* number of spaces on each entry to the method, increasing the indent each time. The resulting printout for a call of *printNumRP(1,7)* looks like the following (note that the line numbers have been added, and are not generated by the code):

```
 1>  Entering printNumR, start= 1
 2>   Entering printNumR, start= 2
 3>    Entering printNumR, start= 3
 4>     Entering printNumR, start= 4
 5>      Entering printNumR, start= 5
 6>       Entering printNumR, start= 6
 7>        Entering printNumR, start= 7
 8>        End of the recursion!
 9>        Exiting printNumR, start= 7
10>       Exiting printNumR, start= 6
11>      Exiting printNumR, start= 5
12>     Exiting printNumR, start= 4
13>    Exiting printNumR, start= 3
14>   Exiting printNumR, start= 2
15> Exiting printNumR, start= 1
```

In this output, it is much easier to see what is happening. In simplified terms, each time any method is called, information about it is pushed onto a system stack structure, including the return address of where it is supposed to resume executing after the call. The same is true for recursive calls. *printNumRP(1,7)* is the first call, resulting in the printout at line 1. Before this first call finishes, it calls itself with *printNumRP(2,7)*, generating line 2. But this then calls *printNumRP(3,7)* to output line 3, and so on, with the stack of unfinished *printNumRP()* calls piling up (so to speak), until the parameter *start* equals the parameter *end* (both are '7'), printing output lines 7 and 8, and stopping the recursion. The remaining output lines, 9 through 15, are printed as the stack of calls unwinds itself with each method completion, and the execution resumes with the previous instance of the method, until the stack is emptied of *printNumRP()* calls.

A Recursive Mathematical Function: *n!*

A common recursion example is the *factorial* function, designated as *n!*, and described as "the product of the integers from 1 to n". Symbolically,

$$n! = 1 \times 2 \times 3 \times ... \times (n-1) \times n$$

so that, for example,

$$5! = 1 \times 2 \times 3 \times 4 \times 5 = 120$$

But there is also a recursive definition which becomes apparent, if one recognizes the relationship:

$$n! = n \times (n-1)!$$

which shows that *n!* may be defined in terms of *(n-1)!*.

Here is a traditional recursive definition of the factorial function:

factorial(0) = 1
factorial(n) = n * factorial(n-1) *for n>=1; otherwise, undefined*

This definition easily translates into a Java implementation, if negative values for *n* are simply treated the same as 0:

```
static int factorial(int n) {
    int result;
    if (n <= 0)
      result = 1;
    else
      result = n * factorial(n-1);
    return result;
}
```

As written this *factorial* method will calculate the correct value for *n!* for values of *n* from 0 up to about 12, because the value of 13! exceeds the storage capacity of the **int** variable. **Unfortunately, Java will not generate any runtime errors if this function is called with *n* > 12, but will happily produce wrong results with no indication whatsoever!** This shows why it is always wise to verify results rather than simply assuming that they are correct.

Rules For Recursion

The most common programmer error when using recursion is the inadvertent creation of an infinite loop through a faulty stopping condition. Referring back to the *factorial()* code, imagine that the `if (n <= 0)` condition is changed to `if (n == 0)`, and *n* is passed with an initial value of -1. In this case, the recursion would never hit a stopping condition because it would never be equal to 0, and it would continue to become more negative as 1 is subtracted on each recursive call. The program would run until the system stack expands to fill the available memory, and then generate a runtime 'stack full' error.

A few rules of thumb help the programmer to code recursive methods which do what they are supposed to do, and stop as intended.

    1) Redefine the problem to be solved, if necessary, so that it is in 'divide and conquer' terms, with a clear statement of an *action* step that can be done to make progress to solving the entire problem, and a *recursive* step that will call the method on a somehow smaller version of the current problem– a shorter list, or a value closer to the stopping point.

    2) Define the stopping condition, based on the statement in (1), which will halt the recursion. Be especially careful to define the conditional so that an unexpected input (like the -1 in the *factorial()* example above) will not skip the condition and result in infinite recursion.

    3) Define the recursive step in the solution, with the useful action that will help solve the problem, and a recursion step on a reduced version of the problem which will definitely move *toward* the stopping condition in (2).

Recursing Through a Linked List

Another practical use of recursion is in stepping through a linked list. First, consider the previously-discussed *Display()* method:

```
    // Display the current list contents, low to high
    public void Display(){
        Node currNode = start;
        System.out.println("List contents:");
        // step through the list
        while (currNode != null) {
            System.out.println(" "+currNode.value);
            currNode = currNode.next;
        }
        System.out.println("------------------");
    }
```

This uses the now-familiar technique of moving through the linked list using:

```
        currNode = currNode.next;
```

inside of the **while** loop to print values until the **null** reference is reached. As an alternative to this iterative approach, the following uses a recursive method:

```
    public void DisplayR(){
        System.out.println("List contents:");
        DisplayRecursive(start);
        System.out.println("------------------");
    }
```

The public method *DisplayR()* takes no parameters, and is accessible through the interface of the linked list. It prints the non-repetitive label at the top of the list, and the final dashed line. In between these two outputs, it calls *DisplayRecursive(start)* to print all of the list contents recursively. The intent is that the calling program can call this public, parameterless *DisplayR()*, without having to access the private *start* field. The *DisplayRecursive()* code:

```
private void DisplayRecursive(Node curr){
   if (curr != null){
     System.out.println(curr.value);
     DisplayRecursive(curr.next);
   }
}
```

is deceptively simple. The strategy is to print the current *Node's* value (the *action* step, and then to print the rest of the list (the *recursive* step). The stopping condition for the recursion is when the *Node* parameter *curr* is **null,** meaning that the end of the list has been reached. If *curr* is not **null**, the *value* located there is printed, and the recursive call is made using *curr.next* as the parameter. It is typical, when using recursion on a linked list, to use a *Node* parameter in the recursive method, and to use a **null** check as the stopping condition to halt the recursion.

Interestingly, this recursive display code can be modified to print the entire list in *reverse* order by simply exchanging two lines:

```
if (curr != null){
   DisplayRecursive(curr.next);
   System.out.println(curr.value);
}
```

In this case the recursion goes forward before the value at *curr* is printed. Written as above, the calls recurse until the **null** *Node* is reached, and then the printing happens, beginning with the last value in the list, and ending with the first value. In comparison, attempting to print the list in reverse *iteratively* would be much more complicated, less efficient, and require more code.

A Recursive Selection Sort

The Selection Sort discussed previously is chosen as a final example of recursion. This sort breaks up naturally into a *divide and conquer* approach: the *action* step is to place the smallest value at the top of the existing list, and the *recursive* step is to then sort all the rest of the list.

```
 1>  public static void ssort(int[] a, int low, int high){
 2>     int i,temp;
 3>     if (low < high){
 4>        for (i=low+1;i<=high;i++)
 5>           if (a[i] < a[low]){
 6>              temp = a[i];
 7>              a[i] = a[low];
 8>              a[low] = temp;
 9>           } //end of for
10>        ssort(a,low+1,high);
11>     } //end if
12>  }
```

The **int** array to be sorted is *a*, and the range of indices to be sorted is from *low* to *high*. On each *ssort* call, the smallest value in the range ends up at index *low* by the processing of the **for** loop, and then the recursive call to *ssort* operates on the shorter part of the array starting at *low+1*. The stopping condition is when *low* and *high* are equal, meaning there are no more values to compare.

As a final recursion example, the following selection sort, *ssort2()*, is presented as the functional equivalent of *ssort()*, but using **no iteration**, instead calling another recursive method, *getmindex()*, to find the smallest value in the remainder of the array.

As in *ssort()*, the stopping condition occurs when *low* and *high* are equal. Otherwise, *mindex* is set to the index of the smallest value in the rest of the array, starting at *low+1*, using a call to *getmindex()*. If *a[mindex]* is smaller than the first element located at *a[low]*, the two slots are swapped. Then, the recursive call to *ssort2()* is made, starting at *low+1*.

```
public static void ssort2(int[] a,int low, int high){
    //recursive sort of a from index low to high
    int mindex,temp;
    if (low< high){
        //get smallest of the rest of the array
        mindex = getmindex(a,low+1,high);
        // put smallest value into a[low]
        if (a[mindex] < a[low]){
          temp = a[mindex];
          a[mindex] = a[low];
          a[low] = temp;
        }
        ssort2(a,low+1,high);
    }
}
```

Getmindex() recursively searches for and returns the index of the smallest value in *a* in the range from *low* to *high*. The *result* is assumed to be *low*. *minrest* saves the result of the recursive call on the remainder of the array. If *a[minrest]* is less than *a[low]*, *result* is updated so that *minrest* is returned.

```
private static int getmindex(int[] a,int low, int high){
//returns index of smallest value in a from low to high
    int result = low; //assume smallest at low
    int minrest;      //min of the rest of the array
    if (low < high){
      minrest = getmindex(a,low+1,high);
      if (a[minrest]< a[low])
        result = minrest;
    }
    return result;
}
```

Chapter Checklist

- ❏ Recursion is not uncommon in everyday life, but it can be difficult to understand because we are much more familiar with iterative problem-solving methods.

- ❏ Certain kinds of problems in computer science are especially well-suited to recursive solutions, as they can be naturally defined recursively.

- ❏ The *divide and conquer* concept is helpful in shaping a recursive problem solution.

- ❏ Recursive method calls in a programming language are possible because at each call, the information needed to return to the caller is pushed onto the system stack, and popped off when the called method finishes executing.

- ❏ Three rules for successfully programming recursively are: 1) State the solution as a *divide and conquer*, approach with an *action* step which solves a small part of the problem, and a *recursive* step which operates on a reduced-size problem; 2) Define the condition needed for stopping the recursion; 3) Define the recursive call which will reduce the problem and move toward the stopping condition.

- ❏ Recursion is useful for many coding objectives: printing a series of values, factorial and other recursive math function calculations, linked list traversal, and sorting arrays.

> **Debugging is twice as hard as writing the code in the first place. Therefore, if you write the code as cleverly as possible, you are, by definition, not smart enough to debug it.**
> *– Brian W. Kernighan*

Chapter 18: Doubly-Linked Lists

One of the difficulties with the singly-linked lists encountered previously is that they only provide one-direction access through the list. The task of moving backwards through the list is naturally awkward and inefficient. In order to improve efficiency in a list where bi-directional access is necessary, it is worthwhile to create both forward and backward links between the nodes.

A Doubly-Linked Node

The doubly-linked list requires a new Node type, named *Node2* here, which has both a *next* reference and a *prev* reference. The *prev* field will be set to point to the previous *Node2* object in the list.

```
public class Node2 {
   int data;
   Node2 next, prev;
   //Constructor
   Node2(int value, Node2 nxt, Node2 pre){
       data = value;
       next = nxt;
       prev = pre;
   }
}
```

The *Node2* constructor includes the *value* to be stored in the object, and the *next* and *prev* references.

Implementing the Doubly Linked List

The *DoubleEndedList* discussed in Chapter 14 was singly-linked. The doubly-linked version uses the same *left* and *right* references to indicate the two ends of the list, but are *Node2* variables. The code which follows implements the doubly-linked version of: *InsertLeft(), RemoveLeft(), InsertRight,* and *RemoveRight()*.

```
void InsertLeft(int n){
    left = new Node2(n, left, null); //adds to left end
    if (right == null)    // the list was empty before
        right = left;
    else                  //set prev of old leftmost
        left.next.prev = left;
}
```

InsertLeft() adds a new *Node2* Node with a **null** *prev* reference, and *next* referencing the old *left Node2*. The *right* reference will be **null** if the list was previously empty, and so is set to the single new *Node2* in the list. Otherwise, the new second *Node2* has its *prev* field set to reference the new *Node2*.

DOUBLY-LINKED LISTS

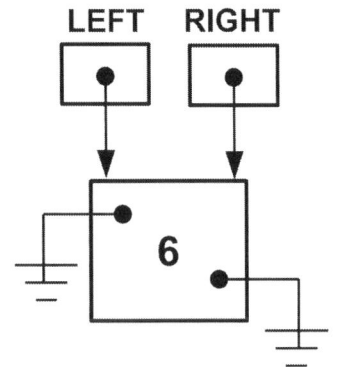

Figure 53 shows the result of the first insertion into the doubly-linked list. Both *left* and *right* refer to this same node, and both its *left* and *right* fields are set **null**. Figure 54 shows the list after *InsertRight(11)* has been called.

The code for *RemoveLeft()* parallels the singly-linked version.

Figure 53: Doubly-linked list after the first node has been inserted

```
int RemoveLeft(){
    int result = left.data;  //save the value
    left = left.next;        //move to next
    if (left == null)        //list is empty
       right = left;
    else
       left.prev = null;     // point back to null
    return temp;
}
```

The *RemoveLeft()* method saves the leftmost node *data* field. Then, *left* is advanced to the *next* reference. If this was the last node being removed, *right* is set to *left*, making both **null**. Otherwise, the new node *prev* field is set to **null**.

In Figure 55, the result of *InsertRight(24)* is shown, with all of the *next* and *prev* fields properly set.

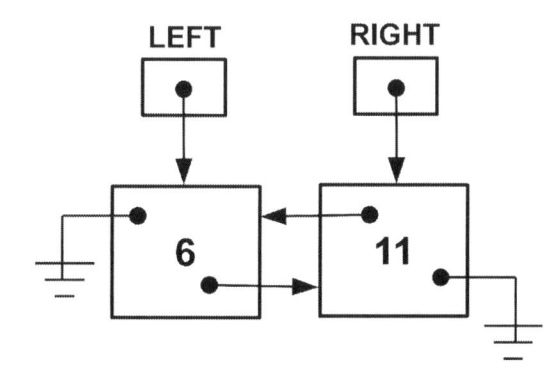

Figure 54: Doubly-linked list after InsertRight(11) call

```
void InsertRight(int n) {
    right = new Node2(n, null, right);
    if (left == null)    //list was empty
        left = right;
    else                 //fix next to last
        right.prev.next = right;
}
```

InsertRight() mimics the action of *InsertLeft()*, with the direction reversed to operate on the opposite end of the list.

DOUBLY-LINKED LISTS

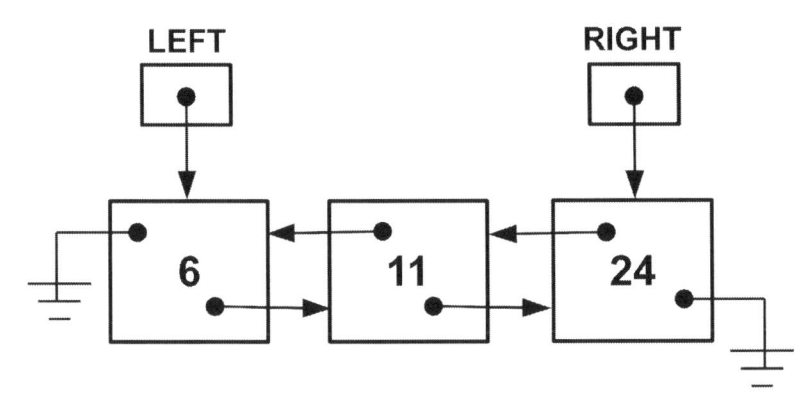

Figure 55: Doubly-linked list after InsertRight(24) call

```
int RemoveRight(){
    int temp = right.data;
    right = right.prev;   //move over
    if (right==null)
        left = right;
    else
        right.next = null;
    return temp;
}
```

RemoveRight() mirrors the operation of *RemoveLeft()*, again with the direction reversed to operate on the opposite end of the list.

Traversing Using the *prev* Field

The following *displayRightToLeft()* method demonstrates moving through the list from right to left:

```java
void displayRightToLeft(){
    Node2 curr = right;
    System.out.print("List R to L: | ");
    while (curr != null){
        System.out.print(curr.data+" | ");
        curr = curr.prev;
    }
    System.out.println();
}
```

The logic starts *curr* at the *right* reference, and advances toward the *left* reference using the *curr=curr.prev* assignment. The **while** loop terminates when the **null** *prev* reference on the left end of the list is reached.

Adding and Deleting Within the List

To complete the doubly-linked list discussion, four methods are described below which support inserting new nodes into the middle of the list, rather than at the ends. First, the *find()* method returns a reference to the node which contains the value *x*.

```java
Node2 find(int x){
    // returns null if x is not in the list,
    // else the reference to node containing x
    boolean found= false;
    Node2 curr = left;
    while ((curr != null)&&(!found)){
        found = (curr.data == x);
        if (!found)
            curr = curr.next;
    }
    return curr;
}
```

The search begins at *left*, and continues until the value is found, or the end of the list is encountered.

After a node reference has been found, the node can be deleted by calling *delete()* with a call like: *delete(find(11))*, which would delete the node containing '11', if it exists. No error will occur if the *find()* result is **null**. Figure 56 illustrates the process.

```
void delete(Node2 n){
   //delete node2 n by rerouting the
   // references on either side of it
   if (n != null){
     if (n.next != null) //n is not at right end
        n.next.prev = n.prev;
     if (n.prev != null) //n is not at left end
        n.prev.next = n.next;
     //fix up left and right if needed
     if (n==left)  //update left, removing leftmost node
        left = left.next;
     if (n==right)
        right = right.prev;
   }
}
```

At the end of the *delete()* call, the local parameter variable *n* is no longer declared, so that the node containing '11' which *n* referenced will be automatically deallocated, along with its *prev* and *next* references to nodes '6' and '24', respectively.

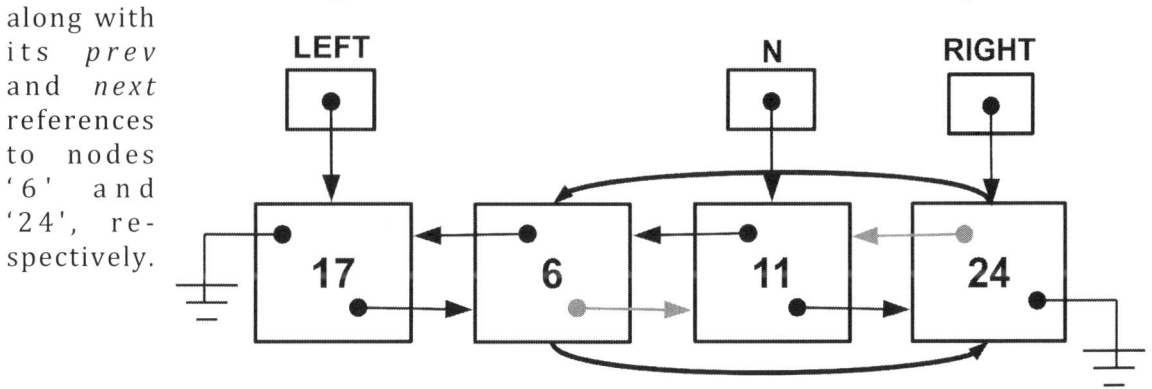

Figure 56: Deletion of node N by redirecting N.next.prev and N.prev.next

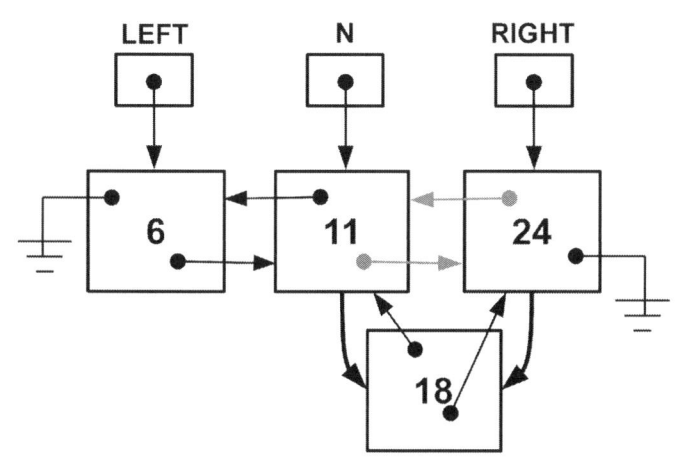

Figure 57: Inserting node '18' after node N by redirecting the next of '11' and prev of '24'

```
void insertAfter(Node2 n, int x){
// Make new node to hold x, add to the RIGHT of node n
   if (n!=null){        //prevent null reference error
     n.next = new Node2(x,n.next,n); //insert new node
     //if not at right end, set prev pointer
     if (n.next.next !=null)
        n.next.next.prev = n.next;
     else                          //added at end, set right
        right = right.next;    //new node is right end
   }
}
```

InsertAfter() creates a new node containing the value *x*, and inserts it into the list after node *n*. As shown in Figure 57, inserting '18' after the node containing '11' with a call like: *insertAfter(find(11),18)* would redirect the *next* field of node '11', and the *prev* field of node '24' to both reference the new '18' node, while setting the node '18' *next* to reference '24' and its *prev* to reference '11'.

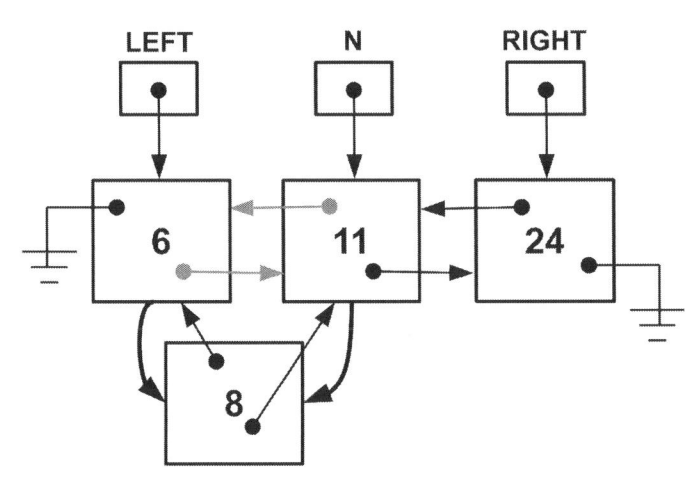

Figure 58: *Inserting node '8' before node N by redirecting the next of '6' and the prev of '11'*

Similarly, the *insertBefore()* method places a new node as the predecessor to a selected node. Using a call like *insertBefore(find(11),8)* would create a node as shown in Figure 58.

```
void insertBefore(Node2 n, int x){
// Make new node to hold x, add to the RIGHT of node n
   if (n!=null){        // prevent null reference error
      n.prev = new Node2(x,n,n.prev); //insert new node
      //if not at left end, set next pointer
      if (n.prev.prev !=null)
         n.prev.prev.next = n.prev;
      else                         //added at end, set left
           left= left.prev;  //new node is left end
      }
   }
```

The code parallels the code of *insertAfter()*, redirecting the *next* field of the '6' node, and the *prev* field of the '11' node to point to the new node containing '8'.

Chapter Checklist

❏ The Doubly-Linked List allows for more efficient traversal of the list from left to right or from right to left.

❏ The *Node2* example of a node containing two different reference fields is typical of this kind of linked list.

❏ Insertion and deletion at the ends of the list are similar to the singly-linked version. Also, insertion into the middle of the list is accomplished by assigning four different references: the *next* and *prev* of the new node, the *prev* of the node following the new node, and the *next* of the node preceding it.

> When you come to a fork in the road,
> take it.
> – *Yogi Berra*

Chapter 19: Binary Trees

In computer science, trees are data structures which are fundamentally hierarchical in their ordering of data. Common examples of trees include a genealogical family tree, a computer file system containing a hierarchy of folders of files and/or other folders, and a corporate organizational chart. Such trees represent an intuitive ordering which indicates some precedence in the ordering of the data. In a family tree, the people represented are ordered by time, with the earlier individuals preceding those born after them. A computer file system organizes data by categories which are meaningful to and defined by the computer user, with more general categories, represented by folders, containing more specific categories. In an organizational chart, the entries are ordered by level or degree of authority and responsibility.

Basic Graph Definitions Related to Binary Trees

A binary tree is specialized tree structure, where each entry has at most two entries directly connected to it. In order to speak unambiguously about binary trees, there are a number of terms to be defined involving a specific usage of certain words. Fortunately, the definitions are intuitive, and easy to understand, and will hopefully be familiar based on past experiences.

Since the binary tree structure represents a graph from mathematical theory, there are six graph-related definitions needed in order to understand the characteristics and connectivity of the tree.

1. A ***graph*** is a set of ***nodes*** or ***vertices*** (usually represented and drawn as circles) and ***edges***, each of which connects one pair of nodes (drawn as lines connecting the circles).

2. A ***directed graph*** has one-directional edges, often drawn with an arrowhead to indicate the direction. A directed edge indicates a one-way relationship between nodes.

3. 2. A ***connected*** graph is one in which there are connecting edges arranged such that any node can be reached from any other node (ignoring the direction of one-way edges if necessary).

4. The ***degree*** of a node simply tells how many edges attach to it. In a directed graph, the ***in-degree*** is the number of edges entering, and the ***out-degree*** is the number of exiting edges.

5. A graph is ***acyclic*** (has no ***cycles***) if there is no way to start at a node, leave via an edge, and follow a sequence of edges to return to the starting node.

6. **Finally,** a ***binary tree*** is a connected, directed, acyclic graph of one or more nodes, where all nodes have *out-degree* of 0, 1, or 2, and *in-degree* of 1, except the ***root node***. One node is designated as the ***root***, or starting point of the tree, and it has *in-degree* of 0. The binary tree is naturally recursive in its definition, as each node in the tree can be considered the root of a subtree consisting of all the nodes connected to it by any outgoing edges. This means that each binary tree, and each of its subtrees, is a tree of subtrees, and particularly suited to recursive algorithms.

Figure 59 shows an example of a typical binary tree. The root of the tree is always drawn at the top of the picture, so that the image is read from top to bottom. The nodes

BINARY TREES

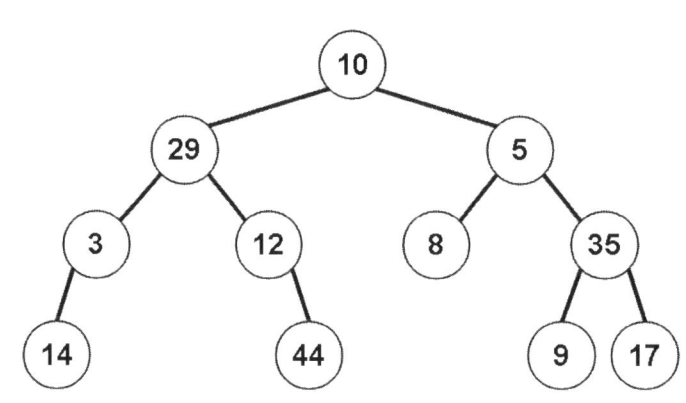

Figure 59: Example of a typical binary tree

appear as circles containing a value which is meaningful to the problem at hand. Edges are drawn without arrowheads, with an implied directionality going from top to bottom. Although each node (except the root) has exactly one edge entering (always attached to the upper half of the circle), the nodes can have zero, one, or two edges exiting (which are always attached to the lower half of the circle).

Binary Tree Terminology

There are several common terms used to describe binary trees and the relationships among the nodes. Many of these are drawn from the analogy of a family tree, with some taken from comparisons to actual, natural trees.

A *path* in a tree is a sequence of edges leading from one node to another.

The *height* of a tree is the longest possible path in the tree, from the root to the most distant node, counting the intervening edges. The height of the tree in Figure 59 is **three**.

The *level* of a node is the number of edges between the root and the node. The root is at Level 0; nodes '29' and '5' are at Level 1; nodes '3', '12', '8', and '35' are at Level 2; nodes '14', '44', '9', and '17' are at the highest level in this tree, Level 3. The highest level in a tree is also the height of the tree.

The *parent* of a node is the one connected to it by an incoming edge. Each node (except the root) has exactly one parent. In Figure 59, for example, '12' is the parent of '44', and '35' is the parent of both '9' and '17'.

A **child** of a node is connected to it by an outgoing edge. Each node may have zero, one, or two children. Referring to Figure 59, '9' and '17' are children of '35', and '29' and '5' are children of '10'. The children of a node are referred to as the **left child** and **right child**, based on their physical location in the drawing.

An **ancestor** of a node is any one which is connected to it higher in the tree. In the Figure, the ancestors of '14' are '3', '29', and '10'. The ancestors of '8' are '5' and '10'. The root of a tree is the ancestor of every other node in the tree.

A **descendant** of a node is any node which is connected to it lower in the tree. Every node is a descendant of the root. The descendants of '5' are '8', '35', '9', and '17'.

A **sibling** of a node is a node that has the same parent. Any node (except the root) can have at most one sibling in a binary tree.

A **leaf** node is one which has no descendants. In Figure 59, the leaf nodes are '14', '44', '8', '9', and '17'.

A **branch** of a tree is any connected set of nodes in the tree.

To **visit** a node, in a computer program, is to make that node the current node under consideration, and perform some operation on the node, such as: to access its data, to print the data, to check its status or number of children, to add its data to some accumulator, or to count the node.

A **traversal** of a tree is the process of *visiting* each of the nodes in the tree. Most often, a traversal is performed according to a pre-defined sequence. The different kinds of traversals will be discussed in **Chapter 21, Tree Traversals**.

BINARY TREES

Binary Tree Applications

There are several variations of binary trees, each differentiated by the particular organizational rules used to order the contained data. The common factor among them is that they generally offer fast searching and efficient insertion and deletion of nodes without the need to relocate data in memory. Because binary tress are recursive in nature, they are well-suited to recursive algorithms.

Chapter Checklist

❏ Binary trees are intuitive, hierarchical data structures which are efficient for searching, and can be implemented to provide the insertion and deletion of nodes without the need to move large amounts of data in memory.

❏ A binary tree is a connected, directed, acyclic graph of one or more nodes, where all nodes have out-degree of 0, 1, or 2, and in-degree of 1, except the root node. One node is designated as the root, or starting point of the tree, and it has in-degree of 0.

❏ There are several terms which are need to speak clearly about trees: *path, height, level, parent, child, ancestor, descendant, sibling, leaf, branch, visit, and traversal.*

❏ Recursive algorithms are particularly simple and effective when dealing with trees.

> Willingness to be taught what we do not know is the sure pledge of growth both in knowledge and wisdom
> – Blair

Chapter 20: The Binary Search Tree (BST)

A Binary Search Tree (BST) is a binary tree which exhibits the **Binary Search Tree Property,** which states that:

At each node in the tree, the sorting value of its right child is greater than the node's value, and the sorting value of its left child is less than the node's value.

The implications of this property can easily be overlooked. Importantly, it provides a high degree of organization to the tree, and allows it to be binary-searched, allowing $O(log_2 n)$ search times if the tree is fully optimized (a topic to be fully discussed later in this chapter). At a very high level, the search process becomes:

Check a node for the search value; if it is equal, stop looking; if the sought value is less than this node's value, look down its left branch, otherwise look down its right branch. Repeat...

This process is repeated for each node encountered, and ultimately the sought value is found, if it is in the BST. Thankfully, the BST is easy to implement using a linked structure which relies heavily on recursive algorithms to simplify the programming logic.

The Binary Tree Node Implementation: *BTNode*

The BST implementation described here is based on a few simple changes to the *Node2* class described previously when implementing the doubly-linked list. The *BTNode* similarly uses two self references, named, appropriately, *left* and *right*, which will be set to point to the node's left and right child nodes. Note that even though the *BTNode* is similar in definition to the *Node2* class, it will be used in a completely different, non-linear structure which has different characteristics from the doubly-linked list.

```
public class BTnode {
   int data;
   BTnode left, right;

   BTnode(int val, BTnode L, BTnode R){
      data = val;
      left = L;
      right = R;
   }
}
```

The *BTNode* constructor sets the **int** data value as well as both of the child-node pointers.

Safely Implementing Recursion in the *BST* Class

The class definition for the *BST* is described below. One of the techniques which appears repeatedly in the method implementations bears a detailed description.

There is a conflict which must be solved. First, the recursive functions which operate on the BST recurse based on a *BTNode* parameter, halting the recursion when the parameter is **null**. However, the *root* field of the BST, indicating the start of the tree, should be protected from outside access by declaring it as **private,** according to the principle of *data hiding*. This means that an outside caller cannot call the recursive methods to start with the *root* node, as is necessary to begin the recursion.

The solution is to create an interface for the *BST* class which allows the *root* to be private, by defining non-recursive **public** method definitions which do not require the *root* as a parameter. For example, searching is initiated using the **public** method *Find(int value)*, which does not require a *BTNode* parameter. *Find* then makes the call to the **private** recursive helper method, *FindR(BTNode n, int value)*, as *FindR(value,root)* to begin the recursive search. Hence, the pattern of a **public** non-recursive method calling a **private** recursive helper method will appear several times. This will become clear when the actual code is discussed below.

Implementing the BST Class *Add()* Method

The start of the *BST* class follows, including the *Add()* method, with descriptions:

```
1  package bstexample;
2  public class BST {
3     //Binary search tree class
4     private BTnode root;
5     //Constructor
6     public BST(){
7        root = null;
8     }
9
```

The *BST* requires only the **private** *root* field, and the constructor simply sets it to **null**.

```
10  //Adds value to the BST without balancing
11  public void Add(int value){
12     if (root == null)     //must create new root
13        root = new BTnode(value,null,null);
14     else                  //recurse using HELPER method
15        AddR(root,value);
16  }
```

The public *Add()* method checks if *root* is **null**, and if so, creates a new node as the tree root. Otherwise, it calls the private recursive helper method *AddR()*.

```
18  //Recursive helper function to add value;
19  // Note: n is NEVER null upon entry
20  private void AddR(BTnode n, int value){
21     if (value < n.data) //must add to the LEFT
22        if (n.left == null)   // no left node yet, add
23           n.left = new BTnode(value,null,null);
24        else                  // left exists, recurse
25           AddR(n.left,value);
26     else  //value >= n.data -- duplicates are allowed
27           //must add to the RIGHT side
28        if (n.right == null)  //no right node yet
29           n.right = new BTnode(value,null,null);
30        else                  // right exists
31           AddR(n.right,value);
32  }
33
```

AddR() is never called with a **null** *n* parameter. If the *value* to be added is less than the current node being considered, the new node will be added somewhere to the left of the current node, to maintain the *Binary Search Tree Property* of the tree (line 21). At line 22, if the left child of *n* is **null**, the new node is created as the new left child (23). Else, a recursive call is made at line 25, with the left child node as the starting point of the next level of recursion. Line 28 is reached only if the new value is greater than (or equal to) the current node's value, meaning that it should be added somewhere to the right of the current node. If the right child is **null**, the new node is created there,

THE BINARY SEARCH TREE (BST)

otherwise the recursion proceeds down the right branch of the current node (line 31). Eventually, the correct spot for the new value will be located, and a new node will be created to hold the value.

It is important to know how this add algorithm operates, and to be able to create a correct BST from a list of data values. It is worth noting that the structure of the tree produced by this algorithm is dependent on the sequence of data values added to the tree. An couple of examples will illustrate.

Suppose that the following seven data values are added to a new BST in the order they appear, from left to right:

10, 8, 15, 3, 2, 11, 9

Figure 60 shows the sequence of steps taken as the tree is modified to accommodate each of the new values that are added. '10' is the first value added, so it becomes the root value. '8' is less than '10', so it must be added to the left of '10'. In Step 3, '15' is greater than '10', so it is added to the right of '10'. Adding '3', in Step 4, the check is first done at the root, where it is less than '10', and because the left child ('8') is not null, the check continues to the left. At node '8', '3' is less, so it must be added to the left. '8' has no left child, so that is where '3' is placed. In Step 5, '2' is added, and it is less than '10', '8', and '3', and is finally located as the left child of '3'. '11' is added in Step 6. It is greater than '10', so it must go to the right of '10', but the right child is already occupied with '15'. Node '15' is next checked, '11' is less and must go to the left of '15', and because that spot is open, the '11' node becomes the new left child of '15'. Finally, in Step 7, the '9' is being added. It is less than '10', so the search goes to the left to node '8'. '9' is greater, and because the right child of '8' is open, '9' becomes the right child of '8'.

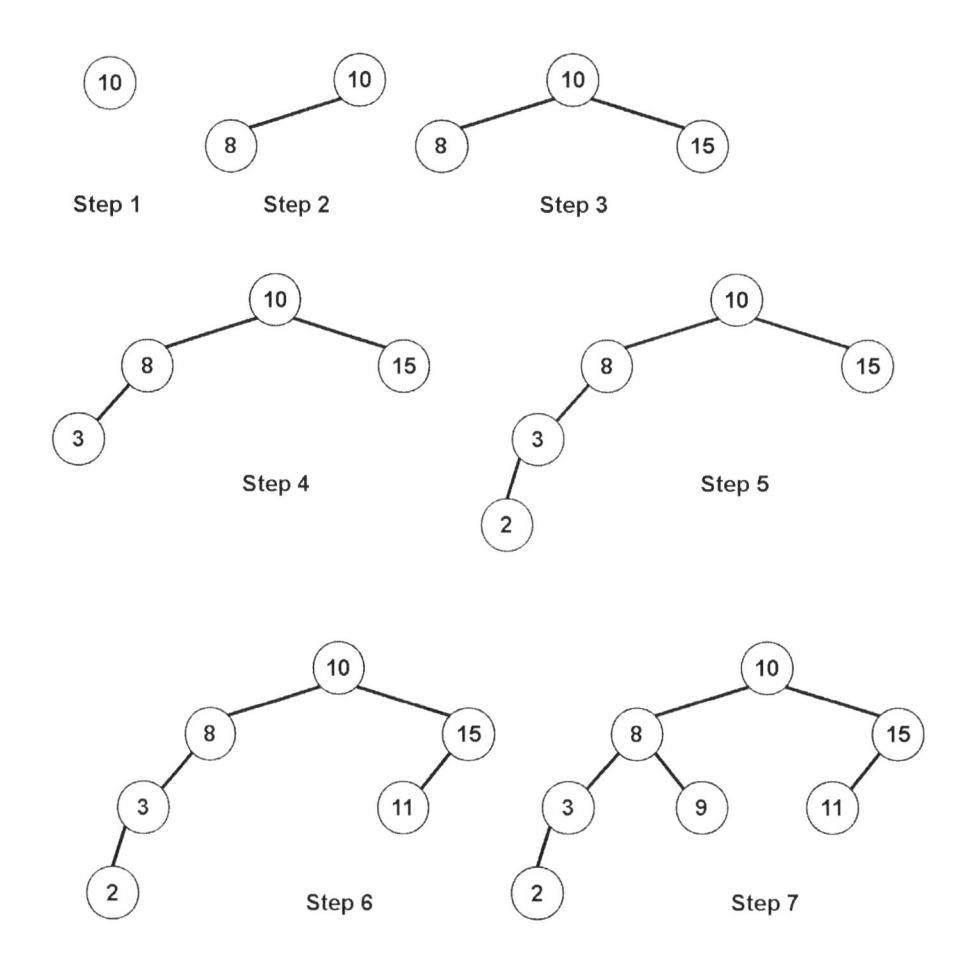

Figure 60: Sequence of changes to a BST as values 10, 8, 15, 3, 2, 11, and 9 are added, in that order

THE BINARY SEARCH TREE (BST)

As stated previously, the sequence in which nodes are added to the BST can drastically affect the final node arrangement. As an illustration, Figure 61 shows the BST which is created if the same values listed above are added in **reverse order**. The sequence now becomes:

9, 11, 2, 3, 15, 8, 10

and the results are quite different. '9', the first value added, automatically becomes the root node. In Step 2, '11' is greater than '9', and must be added to the right of '9'. Step 3 adds '2' by comparing it to the '9' root, and because it is less, it is made the new left child of '9'. The value '3' is added in Step 4. Be-

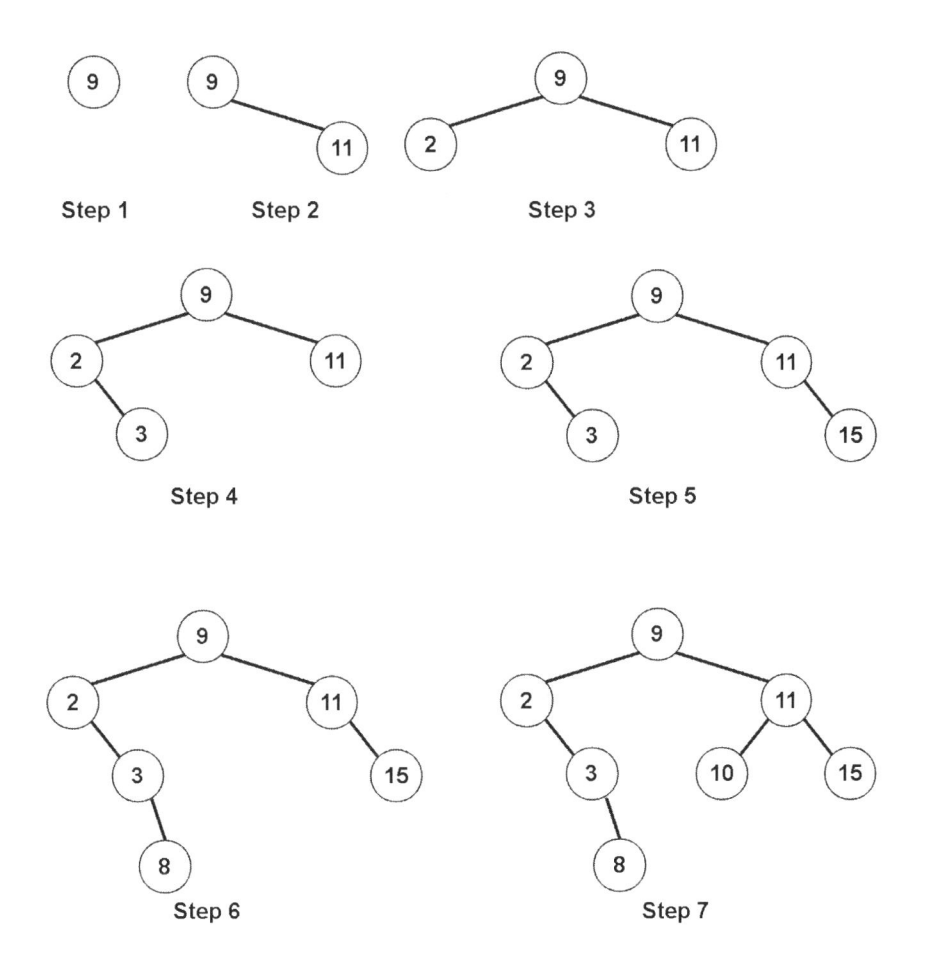

Figure 61: Sequence of changes to a BST as values 9, 11, 2, 3, 15, 8, and 10 are added, in that order

cause it is less than '9', it must go to the left, which is occupied by '2'. Node '2' is compared, and because '3' is greater, and '2' has an open right child, '3' becomes the right child of '2'. In Step 5, '15' is greater than '9', the check goes to the right, and '15' is greater than '11', and since '11' has an open right child, '15' is added there. Step 6 adds the '8' value: it is less than '9', so goes left, is greater than '2', so must go to the right, is greater than '3', and since the right child of '3' is open, it is added there. Step 7 adds the '10', which is greater than '9', and goes to the right, but less than '11', so it ends up as the left child of '11'.

In normal usage, where the sequence of the data values being added is random and fairly evenly distributed across the range of expected values, the algorithm we have been using is perfectly adequate, and will result in a tree which is not very different from the optimal BST discussed in the next section. However, there are some especially poor orderings of the added data which cause the simple algorithm offered here to fail, and produce BSTs which are not efficient for searching. Consider the situation where values are added to the BST already in sorted order, such as with the previous example data:

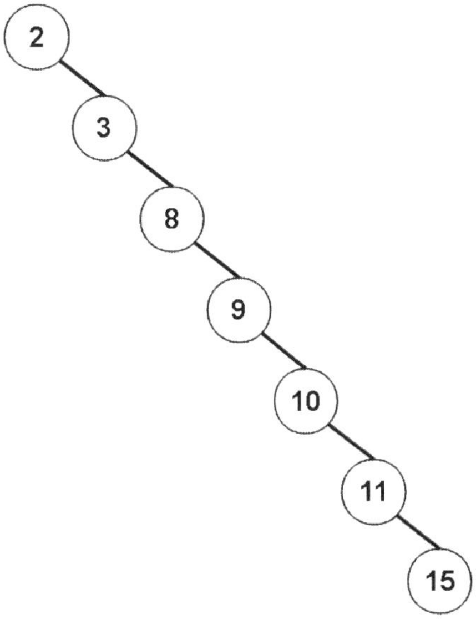

2, 3, 8, 9, 10, 11, 15

One might expect that adding already-sorted data to a data structure which is designed for ordering the data would be a *good* thing. But when these values are added in this sequence, the result is the tree shown in Figure 62. Although this is a valid BST, and it does fulfill the requirements of the *Binary Search Tree Property*, the algorithm did not adapt to the ordering of the input data, and the result is a linear arrangement of the nodes. Such an arrangement of nodes is sometimes referred to as a *degenerate tree*, because although it meets the definition of a tree, and a BST at that, the arrangement of nodes removes the positive benefits of the BST, and results in a

Figure 62: *Degenerate, linear BST resulting from adding values in sorted order*

search time of $O(n)$ rather than the much more attractive $O(log_2 n)$ of the binary search, which was the intent of building the BST in the first place.

There are three obvious ways of dealing with this sequencing problem. First, if the data is available ahead of time, the input sequence could be analyzed to see if it is in sorted or nearly-sorted order. If so, the ordering could be randomized, and the resulting tree would generally be much closer to the ideal tree. Second, again, if the data is known ahead of time, the data could be analyzed in detail, and sequenced to produce the optimal BST, as will be discussed in the next section. Finally, it is possible to add new nodes using an algorithm which re-balances the tree at each add, rearranging the existing nodes as needed to keep the affected branch of the tree as close to the ideal as possible. It turns out that this option is relatively expensive computationally, and relatively complicated to implement, especially if it is invoked for every node added. After discussing the optimal tree for a set of data, an alternative to the constant re-balancing approach is suggested.

The Optimal BST

As suggested earlier, the simple BST add algorithm is effective when the data is added in a random, non ordered sequence. If the BST has been built in this way, even brief sequences of sorted values will not necessarily distort it significantly, and as more randomized values are added, the BST can tend to fill in gaps and correct small problems.

What kind of problems? The question to ask first is, what is an *optimal BST*? When considered in terms of fast searching, it is evident that **the optimal BST is the shortest possible BST which can be constructed from the given data values.** In other words, minimizing the *height* of the BST puts the nodes as close as possible to the root node, and shortens the path to be searched to find a given value. So, the *problems* that can arise in a BST come from having some branches which are substantially longer than the optimal height of the tree. When this happens, search times can be greatly increased as the number of comparisons required to locate a value go up.

Intuitively, the best possible BST for a collection of data is one in which the nodes are most closely packed together, which would be the shortest possible arrangement of the data.

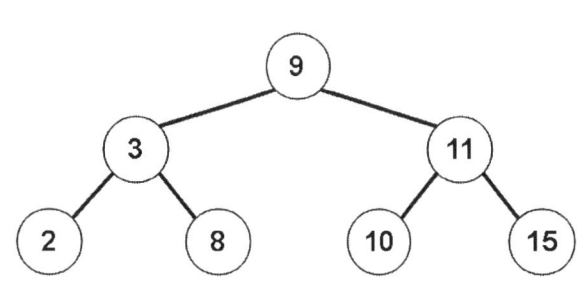

Figure 63 shows the optimal BST for the set of data values shown. It is the shortest possible arrangement of nodes for this data which exhibit the *BST Property*.
A simple iterative algorithm which will generate the optimal BST for a set of data is presented in the following pseudo-code.

Figure 63: *Optimal BST for the given set of data*

1) Sort the data values in ascending order
2) Find the middle (median) value of the set, make this the root
3) Split the data set into two sets-those less than and those greater than the median
4) Find the middle of the lesser data set, add this as the left child node of the root, and split this data set as in (3)
5) Find the middle of the greater data set, add this as the right child of the root, and split this data set as in (3)
6) Repeat 4 and 5 on each subset created, always adding the median of the lesser subset as the left child of the previous median, and the median of the greater subset as the right child

Using this approach, an optimal BST for the consecutive numbers 1 through 11 works as follows. The middle of the 11 values is 6, dividing the data like:

1 2 3 4 5 | 6 | 7 8 9 10 11

The middle value becomes the root node, and the two resulting subsets are divided and treated separately. The lesser subset divides as:

THE BINARY SEARCH TREE (BST)

1 2 | 3 | 4 5

So that '3' becomes the left child of the root, and for the greater subset:

7 8 | 9 | 10 11

the '9' becomes the right child of the root. Figure 64 shows the partial BST at this point. The lesser subset divided by '3' contains the two values:

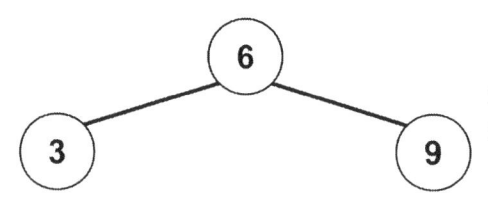

Figure 64: First three nodes in optimal 11 node tree

1 2

The 'middle' of two nodes is arbitrary, but choosing the left puts '1' as the left child of 3, and '2' and the right child of '1'. The greater subset divided by '3' contains:

4 5

and again, '4' is chosen as the 'root' of the subtree, with '5' as its right child. The result is shown in Figure 65.

The right half of the tree is similarly constructed, with

7 8 and **10 11**

becoming the left subtree and right subtrees of the subtree rooted at '9'. The final result is shown in Figure 66. This is as short as any binary tree containing 11 nodes can be constructed. It should be pointed out that this 'optimal' tree is not unique, and would have a slightly different, but inconsequential, arrangement of the nodes. For example, '8' could have been placed as a subtree root in place of '7', with '7' as the left child of '8'. What determines that the BST is optimized is the fact that no shorter tree containing the same data could be constructed, and that each of the levels of the BST above the lowest level are completely filled in with no gaps, thus minimizing the number of nodes which are at the maximum depth.

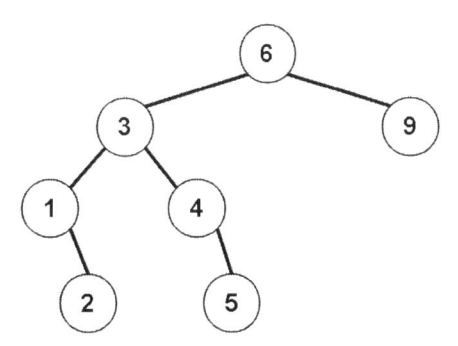

Figure 65: Left half of optimal BST completed

Implementing the BST *Find()* Method

The public *Find()* method takes a single parameter:

```
34  //Search for value in the tree using BINARY SEARCH
35  //Returns null if not found, else the node reference
36  public BTnode Find(int value){
37     BTnode result = null;
38     //Search if tree has any nodes in it
39     if (root != null) {
40        result = FindR(root,value);
41     }
42     return result;
43  }
44
```

The default return is **null**, in case the tree is empty. If *root* is not **null**, the result of the recursive *FindR()* call is returned as the result.

THE BINARY SEARCH TREE (BST)

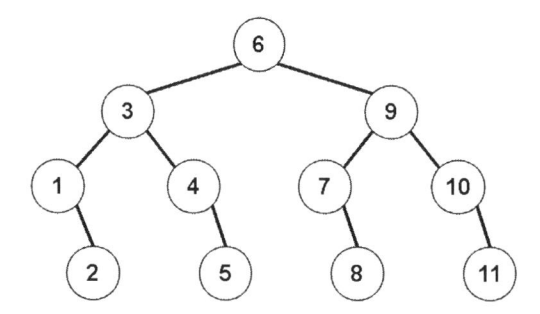

Figure 66: Final optimized BST for 11 nodes

```
45  //Recursive helper for Find, with node parameter
46  private BTnode FindR(BTnode n, int value){
47      BTnode result = null;
48      //If not null, value might be found here
49      if (n !=null) {
50          //if data matches value
51          if (n.data == value)
52              result = n;
53          else
54              // Search to left if value smaller
55              if (value < n.data)
56                  result = FindR(n.left,value);
57              else
58                  // value > n.data, search to right
59                  result = FindR(n.right,value);
60      }
61      return result;
62  }
```

The recursive helper uses the *BST Property* of the tree to direct its search for the *value* parameter. If node parameter *n* is **null**, then the search down the current branch is terminated, and the default **null** is returned. Otherwise, if the *data* field of *n* matches the search *value*, *n* is set as the result, and the search is terminated successfully. If the value has not yet been found, the recursion takes place down the left branch of the tree if the *value* is less than *n.data*. Otherwise, the recursion moves down the right branch.

At each level of the recursion, the result of the further recursion, if required, is returned, so that wherever the value is found, the node reference is passed back up through the recursive calls, and is finally returned to the original caller of the public *Find()* method.

Two More Tree Definitions: *Complete* and *Full*

As seen in the examples presented, trees can technically be constructed with a number of different structures using the same data, with resulting changes in their search efficiencies. A 'linear' (*degenerate*) BST does not possess the desired search characteristics found in a well-balanced tree, where the nodes are close to each other. This leads to two definitions which describe the most desirable BST arrangements or structures. Some books define these terms differently, or flip their meanings, but here, these terms will be used consistently as described below.

A **complete binary tree** is one which has the minimum height $(log_2(n))$ for its size (number of nodes, *n*), and every level is filled, except possibly its highest level which is in from left to right with no gaps. By this definition, the example in Figure 66, while *optimal* as a BST, is not *complete*. Figure 67 shows a *complete* arrangement of the same nodes in a BST, which is also optimal.

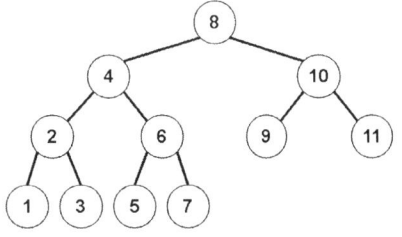

Figure 67: Complete BST with 11 nodes

THE BINARY SEARCH TREE (BST)

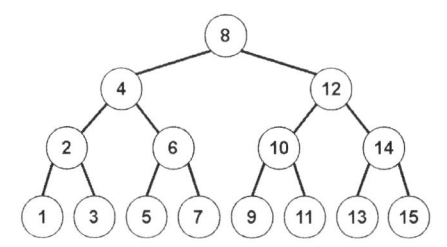

Figure 68: Full BST with 15 nodes

A ***full binary tree*** is a *complete binary tree* which contains **2^n-1** nodes, *(for n > 0)*, so that its highest level is completely filled in. Figure 68 shows a *full* BST containing the values 1 through 15 in its fifteen nodes. Note that every ***full*** tree must, by definition, have a size of 2^n-1. Therefore, the only full trees possible will have node counts of 1, 3, 7, 15, 31, 63, and so on. ***Every full tree is also a complete tree, but every complete tree is not necessarily a full tree.***

More BST Methods

So far, the *Add()* and *Find()* methods have been discussed in this chapter, along with explanations of how the BST works in general. Having established this much, two other areas of BST functionality are addressed in the coming chapters:
    1) methods of traversing a BST, and
    2) the somewhat complex process of deleting nodes from a BST while maintaining the *BST Property*.

Chapter Checklist

- ❏ The Binary Search Tree (BST) is a common Binary Tree variant, with its chief characteristic being that it organizes data for efficient searching. It maintains the *BST Property* at every node, such that its left child is always less than the node's value, and the right child is always greater than (or equal to, if duplicates are allowed) the node.

- ❏ A simple *Add()* algorithm is suitable for the most common real-world situation where the data values are unsorted, and well-distributed across the possible range of values. The algorithm should be understood, so that the resulting, unique BST for a given sequence of added data values can be manually constructed on paper.

- ❏ The optimal BST for a set of data is not necessarily unique, but it is the shortest possible BST that can be constructed, and it has the fewest possible nodes located on the highest level of the BST.

- ❏ The *Find()* method also works well as a recursive method, directing the path of its search using the *BST Property*, so that it only checks the possible locations of the search value, which, optimally, it is able to do in **$O(log_2 n)$** time.

- ❏ A **complete** binary tree has minimal height for the number of nodes it contains *($log_2(n)$)*, with all its levels filled, except its highest level (bottom-most level in drawings), which may not be filled, but is arranged without gaps, from left to right.

- ❏ A **full** binary tree is a complete binary tree containing 2^n-1 nodes, so that all its levels are filled in.

> I shall be telling this with a sigh
> Somewhere ages and ages hence:
> Two roads diverged in a wood, and I—
> I took the one less traveled by,
> And that has made all the difference.
> – *Robert Frost*

Chapter 21: Tree Traversal

A traversal of a binary tree is the process of visiting all of its nodes. There are multiple ways to accomplish the task, and different orders in which to visit the nodes. Three common orderings are of particular interest to the computer scientist: *pre-order, in-order,* and *post-order*, each of which are described and implemented below.

The *pre-order* traversal visits the current node *before* visiting its left and right branches, the *in-order* visits the left branch, then the node, then its right branch in sequence, and the *post-order* visits the left branch, then the right branch, and then the node *after* all its descendants have been visited. All three of these algorithms are easily implemented as recursive methods.

The Pre-order Traversal

In order to remember the sequence of nodes visited for a pre-order traversal, think: **node, left, right**. The pre-order traversal code looks like:

```
void preorder(BTnode n){
    if (n != null){
        visit(n);
        preorder(n.left);
        preorder(n.right);
    }
}
```

The recursion stops whenever a **null** node is encountered. The *visit()* method can be as complex as necessary, but often is as simple as:

```
void visit(BTnode n){
    System.out.println(n.data);
}
```

The beauty of this traversal lies in its simplicity. The node *n* is visited first, with *visit()* taking care of any needed processing of the node. Then, the same process is carried out starting at *n.left,* and then at *n.right.*

Figure 69 shows an un-sorted binary tree. The pre-order traversal would visit the nodes in the following sequence:

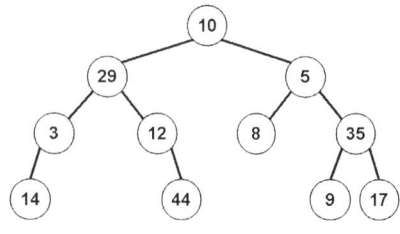

10, 29, 3, 14, 12, 44, 5, 8, 35, 9, 17

Figure 69: A binary tree to be traversed

The result is clear if it is remembered that upon arrival at a node, *exactly the same sequence* takes place each time. The traversal starts at the root, '10'. Visit '10', then pre-order its left branch. Advance to '29', visit, traverse its left branch. This visits '3', then traverses *its* left branch, starting at '14'. '14' is visited, then its left branch, which is null, and then its right branch, also null. The recursion unwinds back to '3', where its right branch would be traversed, but it is null. The recursion returns to '29', already visited, and ready for its right branch to be traversed. '12' is visited, then its left branch would be traversed, but it is null. Its right branch is not null, so '44' is visited next, then its two null branches are traversed, and this completes the processing of the left branch of the root, '10'. The process continues through the right branch, resulting in the sequence shown above.

The In-order Traversal

To recall the sequence here, think: **left, node, right**. The code for the in-order traversal is:

```
void inorder(BTnode n){
    if (n != null){
        inorder(n.left);
        visit(n);
        inorder(n.right);
    }
}
```

The similarity to the pre-order traversal is obvious, but the details of the differences are most important. The *inorder()* method recurses **before** it visits the node it starts at, going as far to the left as possible before actually visiting any node. When the left branch has been traversed, the start node is visited, and then the right branch is traversed in-order. The result sequence of visits for the in-order traversal is:

14, 3, 29, 12, 44, 10, 8, 5, 9, 35, 17

Figure 70 repeats Figure 69 for ease of tracing the traversal. The recursive calls to *inorder(n.left)* continue until the **null** left child of '14' is encountered. Next, '14' is visited, then its **null** right child stops that level of recursion. Processing returns to visit node '3', then the **null** right child of '3' is encountered, returning processing to '29', which is now visited. Its right child, '12', first has its **null** left child checked, then

'12' is visited, then '12's right child, '44', is in-order traversed. Processing returns now to the root, '10', which is visited, before its right branch is in-order traversed. It should be noted that **the in-order traversal of any BST visits the nodes in sorted sequence.**

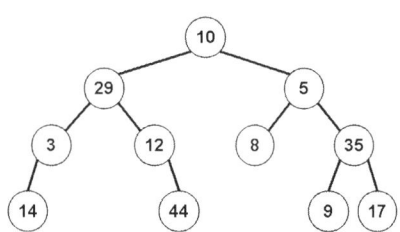

The Post-order Traversal

Figure 70: *A binary tree to be traversed*

The post-order traversal visits: **left, right, node**. This is probably the most difficult traversal to picture, because the visiting of each node is deferred until both of its subtrees have already been traversed. The code parallels the previous two traversals:

```
void postorder(BTnode n){
    if (n != null){
        postorder(n.left);
        postorder(n.right);
        visit(n);
    }
}
```

The post-order traversal of the tree in Figure 70 visits the nodes in the sequence:

> 14, 3, 44, 12, 29, 8, 9, 17, 35, 5, 10

The root is always the last node visited in a post-order traversal. At each node, the left and right branches are traversed before the node is visited. Starting at the root, its left, '29', cannot be visited until its left and right are traversed. The recursion continues down, finally ending with the **null** left and right of '14', which is the first node visited. '3' has no right, so it is visited next. The right of '29' is traversed next, then the left and right of '12', finally reaching '44', the next visited. '12' is finally visited, completing the right of '29' so that it can be visited. Processing continues down the right branch of the root, in the sequence shown, until the root, '10', is visited last.

Another Example of the Traversals

The tree in Figure 71 is presented for further practice. The sequences of nodes visited by the three traversals are:

       PRE-ORDER: 1, 8, 6, 3, 9, 4, 5, 7, 2, 18, 13

       IN-ORDER: 8, 3, 6, 9, 1, 7, 5, 4, 18, 2, 13

       POST-ORDER: 3, 9, 6, 8, 7, 5, 18, 13, 2, 4, 1

Applications of the Traversals

As mentioned previously, an in-order traversal of a BST visits the nodes in sorted order, hence the source of the 'in-order' name. While printing the nodes of a tree in order can be useful, some other uses of the traversal are presented next.

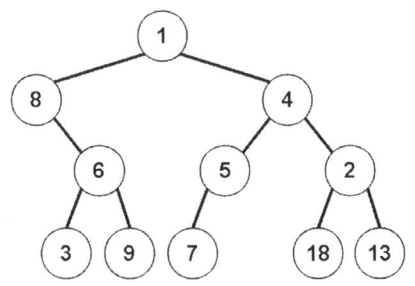

Figure 71: *Example binary tree for traversals*

Finding the Tree Height

First, consider the problem of finding the height of a tree. The height must be determined by visiting each node, and noting its level, and finally returning the highest level reached during the traversal. This may seem difficult at first glance, but the magic of recursion actually makes the process fairly simple. The recursive way of thinking about the problem is, from the perspective of a given node in the tree, 'The height of the tree under me the greater of the nodes under my left and right branches, and their starting level to count from begins at my actual level.' The public interface code is:

```
public int height(){
   return heightR(root, -1);
   }
```

where *height()* simply returns the result of the recursive helper function *heightR()*. The motivation, once again, it to prevent the public method from requiring access to the private *root* field. The *heightR()* method below implements a *pre-order* traversal of the tree, dealing with the node first, then its left branch, then its right branch.

```
private int heightR(BTnode n, int level){
   int result = level; //if null, no change
   if (n!= null)
      result = Math.max(
                  heightR(n.left,level+1),
                  heightR(n.right, level+1));
   return result;
}
```

heightR() recurses based on the node *n*. The initial call *heightR(root, -1)* is designed to account for the possibility of an empty tree, in which case -1 is returned, indicating that a non-existent tree has no height. A tree with a single node, the root, should have a height of 0, which is what happens here. The *result* is set to the incoming *level* by default. If *n* is **null**, it means there is no deeper path here, and the level remains as it is. If *n* is not **null**, then the current level is one greater than it was previously. The height of this branch is thus the maximum of the left branch and the right branch of this node. *level + 1* is passed in the recursive argument to say, in effect, 'The level at this point is what it was above me, plus one, so see if your branch can add on to it'.

Finding the Size of a Tree

Counting the number of nodes in a tree consists of visiting each node and adding to the total. Thinking about this recursively, again from the perspective of a particular node, the solution is something like, 'The size of my part of the tree is a count of 1 for me plus the size of my left branch plus the size of my right branch.' The public interface:

```
public int size(){
   return sizeR(root);
}
```

simply calls the recursive *sizeR(root)*. This is also a *pre-order* traversal, dealing with the node, then its left branch, then its right branch. The order of traversal could be changed by rearranging the recursive calls in the *result* assignment statement:

```
private int sizeR(BTnode n){
   int result = 0; //in case null
   if (n != null){
      result = 1 + sizeR(n.left)+sizeR(n.right);
   }
   return result;
}
```

If *n* is **null** *result* will remain 0, as there is no node present to count. Otherwise, the count of 1 for node *n*, plus the size of each of its two branches, is returned.

An Exhaustive Search

Although the BST makes searching more efficient, there are times, such as with an unordered tree, that an exhaustive search is needed. This kind of search checks through all the nodes in the tree, if necessary, until the value is found. Ideally, it stops as soon as the sought-after value is found, rather than needlessly further traversing the tree. Thinking recursively about the solution, a node perspective might say, 'To find the search value, first check my data value. If I have that value, return my reference. If I do not have that value, first check and see if it is located down my left branch, and if so return the node found. If that search fails, check down my right branch, and return that node if it is successful. If none of these searches is successful, return null back to my caller.'

The public interface calls the recursive helper:

```
public BTnode findExhaustive(int value){
    return findExR(root, value);
}
```

The recursive method performs a *pre-order* traversal of the tree, checking for *value* at each node along the way.

```
private BTnode findExR(BTnode n, int value){
    BTnode result = null;
    if (n != null) {
        if (n.data == value)
            result = n;
        else {
            result = findExR(n.left, value);
            if (result == null)
                result = findExR(n.right, value);
        }
    }
    return result;
}
```

The recursion stops whenever a **null** node is encountered. For non-null nodes, *n.data* is compared to *value*, and if they are equal, the current node *n* is returned, no further recursion occurs, and ultimately is passed up the recursive call sequence, back to the publicly interfaced method.

If *value* is not stored at node *n*, the search continues recursively through the left branch of *n*. Within the **else**, the first recursive call sets *result* to the value returned by recursing down the left branch at *n.left*. If this is not **null**, it was successful and, very important, no further searching is needed. However, if the left-branch search failed, and returns **null**, *result* is updated to the result of searching the right branch under *n*, and this is the result passed up the recursive call sequence.

Chapter Checklist

- The Pre-order traversal of a tree visits the node first, then traverses its left branch, then traverses its right branch. Remember: **node, left., right**, and **pre- means before, the node is visited before its branches.**

- The In-order traversal visits the left branch, the node, then the right branch in left-to-right order. Remember: **left, node, right**, and **looking at the node, the visitation occurs in order, left to right.**

- The Post-order traversal visits the left branch, the right branch and finally, the node. Remember: **left, right, node**, and **post- means after, the node is visited after its branches.**

- Three recursive traversal applications are discussed: *height()*, which determines the height of the tree; *size()*, which counts the number of nodes in the tree; and *findExhaustive()*, which does an exhaustive search through the tree, checking every node until the value is found, or all the nodes have been checked. Each of these are implemented as simple recursive methods which are short and easy to understand.

> **Measuring programming progress by lines of code is like measuring aircraft building progress by weight.**
> *— Bill Gates*

Chapter 22: Deletion in the BST

Having covered the insertion into the BST, searching in the BST, and tree traversals in general, the discussion would be incomplete without describing the deletion of a node from the BST. Because there is some complexity involved, this chapter is devoted to a walkthrough of the deletion process, and the code that makes it work.

Three Different Deletion Cases

The actual deletion of a node ranges from easy to more complex, depending on how the node is connected within the BST. The three possible cases are:
    1) the node has no children
    2) the node has one child
    3) the node has two children

This discussion assumes that the BST shown in Figure 72 exists, and the various kinds of deletions will be illustrated using it as the initial starting point.

It is easy to see that a BST leaf node, which has no child nodes connected with it, is

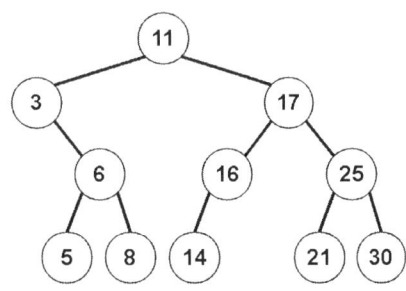

Figure 72: BST for deletion discussion

easy to delete by removing the reference to it from its parent node. In Figure 72, the leaf nodes '5', '8', '14', '21', and '30' would all be simple to delete, as they have no effect on any of the other nodes in the tree– no other node is dependent upon any of them. Figure 73 shows the BST after the removal of node '14' as an example.

The second situation is when the node to be deleted has just one child attached to it. In the BST of Figure 72, this would apply to nodes '3' and '16'. Regardless of the complexity of the subtree under the node to be deleted, the deleted node may be simply replaced by its single child node, while keeping the child's children intact. Figure 74 shows the tree resulting from the deletion of both node '3' and node '16'. It is clear that the resulting tree still exhibits the *BST Property*.

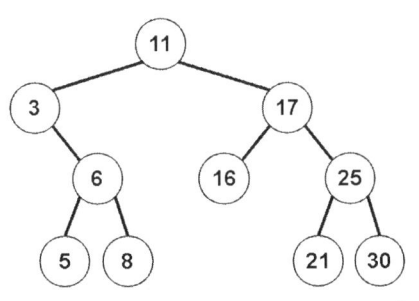

Figure 73: BST after deletion of leaf node 14

The difficult deletion situation occurs when a node has two children. Intuitively, this means that the node is more intricately connected to the rest of the BST, and its deletion requires additional node manipulation. The rule to be followed is straightforward, though it requires some slightly complicated code to accomplish the task.
Consider the original BST of Figure 72, and the deletion of node '17', which has two subtrees as its left and right children. The deletion is made simpler when it is recognized that the node which should replace such a node as '17' is its *in-order successor*, the node which would be visited next in an in-order traversal of the tree. This may seem difficult to find at first, but **the in-order successor is always the left-most descendent of the right child of a node.**

If the right child of a node has no left child, it is, itself, the successor. If it has a left subtree, then following the left of the left of the left, and so on, will finally end at the in-order successor of the original node. In Figure 75, the successor of '17' is node '21'.

DELETION IN THE BST

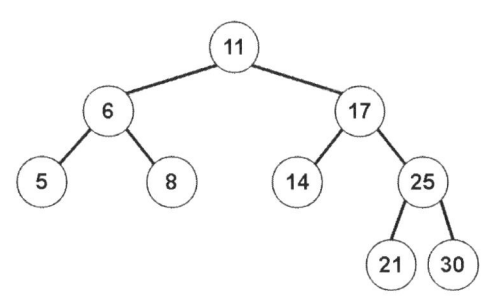

Figure 74: BST of Figure 72 after deletion of '3' and '16'

Another important fact is, **the successor never can have a left child**. Logically, if it did have a left child, that child would be the successor instead of the successor already identified. At this point, the deletion can be described as follows:

1) Find the in-order successor node. This is the node which will replace the deleted node. (In the example, the successor is '21'.)

2) Make the left-subtree of the deleted node the new left subtree of the successor node. Remember, the successor will never have a left subtree. (In the example, '16' is made the left child of '21'.)

3) If the successor was **not** the right child of the deleted node, then make the successor's right subtree, if it exists, the left subtree of the successors parent. This is represented by the node marked 'X' in Figure 75. It does not matter how complex the 'X' subtree is, this still works. If the successor **is** the right child of the deleted node, there is nothing else to be done, as it had no left subtree. (In the example, 'X', the right subtree of '21', becomes the left child of '25'.)

4) Replace the deleted node with the successor node, making the right subtree of the deleted node the right subtree of the successor node, and making the deleted node's parent reference the successor node. (In the example, '11' references '21', and '25' becomes the right child of '21'.)

Implementing the Deletion Code

The actual code for the deletion is somewhat complex, but is broken down into helper methods which aid in understanding how it all works.

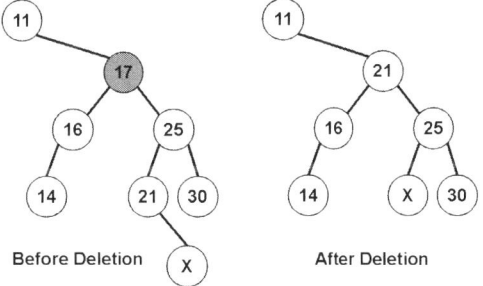

Figure 75: Deletion of node 17

The approach taken here is to present the main delete method first, followed by its various helper functions. The intent is to let *Delete()* present itself somewhat abstractly, with the helper functions simply assumed to do what the comments say, and then to fill in those details for each of the helpers.

The *Delete()* method:

```
141  // BST delete is complex.  Returns
142  //   the reference to the deleted node
143  //   if it is found, otherwise, returns null
144  public BTnode Delete(int value) {
145     BTnode result = null;        //default return
146     BTnode delnode = Find(value);//node w/value to delete
147     BTnode leftBranch = null;//delnode left child
148     BTnode rightBranch = null;//delnode right child
149     BTnode movedNode = null;   //replaces delnode
150     BTnode parent = null;      //parent, delnode
151                                //parent, delnode successor
152     BTnode successorParent = null;
153     boolean isLeft = false;   //true if delnode is left
154                               // child of its parent
155     boolean rootIsDelNode = false; // true if root is
156                                    //  node to delete
```

A number of variables are introduced to keep track of the various references so that no part of the subtrees gets lost along the way. The names are self-descriptive, and the code comments help clarify. The node to be deleted, *delnode*, is established using the *Find()* method described in the BST chapter, and searching for *value* (line 146). *result* will ultimately be the reference to the deleted node. *leftbranch* and *rightbranch* will hold the references to *delnode's* left and right children. *movedNode* is the node that will replace *delnode*, *parent* is *delnode's* parent, and *successorParent* is the parent found for the in-order successor node.

DELETION IN THE BST

```
157      if (delnode != null) {//node w/value WAS found
158          result = delnode;  //save return reference
159          rootIsDelNode = (delnode == root); //check root
160          if (!rootIsDelNode) {  //root is not delete node
161              parent = FindParent(delnode); //find its parent
162              isLeft = (parent.left == delnode);//child?
163          }
164          // save delnode's children
165          leftBranch = delnode.left;
166          rightBranch = delnode.right;
```

If a node containing *value* was found, *delnode* will not be **null**, and *result* is set to reference it. If the *root* node is being deleted, a boolean is set to ensure that *root* is properly changed at the end. Otherwise, *parent* is set to the parent of *delnode*, and *isLeft*, a boolean, is set so that it is known whether *parent's* right or left child must be reset at the end. Finally, *delnode's* children are saved for later transplant into the replacing node.

```
167          // delete action differs w/number of children
168          switch (numberOfChildren(delnode)) {
169          case 0: //no children, no changes,
170                  //parent reference will be set to
171                  // null movedNode
172              break;
173
```

A **switch** statement determines which actions will be taken based on the number of children *delnode* has. The helper method *numberOfChildren* returns this value. If *delnode* has no children, all of the information needed to replace its parent's reference is known, and the parent will finally reference the **null** *modedNode*.

```
174                case 1: //1 child, move the child to
175                        //  its grandparent at end,
176                        //  after picking left/right
177                   if (leftBranch != null)
178                      movedNode = leftBranch;
179                   else
180                      movedNode = rightBranch;
181                   break;
182
```

If *delnode* has one child, the *movedNode* which will replace it is simply set to the non-null child, either the left or right branch saved earlier. Again, *parent* ends up referencing *movedNode*.

```
183                case 2:  //2 children
184                        //since 2 children, successor not null
185                   movedNode = inorderSuccessor(delnode);
186                   // successors's left is always null,
187                   // so it can receive the old left branch
188                   movedNode.left = leftBranch;
189                   // find current parent of node being moved;
190                   //  cannot be null because successor must
191                   //  have parent
192                   successorParent = FindParent(movedNode);
```

Now comes the complex case, when *delnode* has two children. The *movedNode* is set to the result of the *inorderSuccessor()* helper method. Since it is known that the in-order successor can never have a left child, the left child of *delnode*, stored as *leftBranch*, is assigned to it. Finally, the parent of the successor node is assigned into *successorParent* by another helper method.

```
193      // successor of delnode will either be its right child
194      //  (if right child had no left branch) OR  a node in
195      //   the right child's left branch
196      // if succesor is not delnode's right child,
197      //     successorParent gets successors's right branch
198      //    as its own left- OK because
199      //    successor WILL ALWAYS BE successorParent's
200      //    left child
201      //  AND, being moved up to replace delnode, it will
202      //    become ancestor of successorParent
203              if (movedNode != delnode.right) {
204                  //=> delnode isn't successorParent
205                  // replace successor movedNode
206                  //   (always left child of its parent)
207                  // with its right branch on parent's left
208                  successorParent.left = movedNode.right;
209                  // successor gets delnode's right branch
210                  movedNode.right = rightBranch;
211                  // else do nothing;
212   // Note: if successorParent IS delnode, successor
213   //   was delnode's right child; do nothing,
214   //   as successor will replace its own parent
215              }
216       }    //end of switch stmt
217    }     //end of if (delnode != null}
```

There are a number of useful inline comments in the code above. If the replacement node, *movedNode* (here, the successor node) is not directly attached to *delnode* as its right child, then the parent of *movedNode, successorParent* has an open left child, and receives *movedNode's* right subtree. Then, it is safe to set *movedNode's* right to be *delnode's* right branch.

```
218     // Attach movedNode to Parent,
219     // placing it into its final position
220     if (rootIsDelNode)
221         root = movedNode;
222     else
223         if (isLeft)
224             parent.left = movedNode;
225         else
226             parent.right = movedNode;
227     //remove deleted node's child references
228     result.left = null;
229     result.right = null;
230     return result;
231 }
```

The final step in the add process is attaching the already-finished *movedNode* to its parent. If it is the root being deleted, *root* is set to *movedNode* (line 221). Otherwise, *isLeft* indicates whether to update *parent.left* or *parent.right*. As the final actions, and to make sure there are no future unintended links to other tree nodes, the children of *result* (same as *delnode*) are set **null**.

A Design Note

It is worth pointing out that the *Delete()* method above was designed before coding, with the various helper functions treated *abstractly*, as methods which would do a certain function and return the needed data type, without concern for the details of how they would function. By concentrating on *what* they would do, rather than precisely *how* they would accomplish their tasks, it was possible to design *Delete()* before any of the needed helper functions even existed.

This is a powerful concept in problem solving and program design. Often, it is most efficient and effective to start laying out the logic of the solution, such as a BST *Delete()* method, working through each step of what only that method must do. Whenever the designer hits the need for a complicated task like, 'Here, we need to find the in-order successor,' the details of this sub-task are ignored, and an abstract *inorderSuccessor()* method is imagined. The designer may jot down some notes like: *inorderSuccessor(n) must find and return the reference to the node which is the successor of n.* Then, this method may be freely used within the design, as needed, with the assumption that its implementation is an unnecessary detail that can be ignored as the rest of the *Delete()* method is designed. This is repeated for other helper methods, until all of the logic of *Delete()* is worked out and mentally tested for correctness and completeness. When the designer is satisfied that this is the case, the other helper methods can be considered and designed, one at a time.

Implementing the Helper Methods

The helper methods described below generally locate certain existing nodes in the BST which are related to the deletion algorithm. Each of these is an example of breaking a task into smaller pieces which are easy to solve individually.

```
64  //leftmost of node n:
65  // follow left child chain
66  // as far as possible, returning
67  // the last one reached;
68  // if n has no left children, n IS the leftmost
69  private BTnode Leftmost(BTnode n){
70      BTnode result = null;
71      if (n != null){
72          // if left path continues, follow
73          if (n.left != null)
74              result = Leftmost(n.left);
75          // else end of path is reached
76          else
77              result = n;
78      }
79      return result;
80  }
```

The *Leftmost(BTnode n)* method locates and returns the leftmost descendant of the node *n*. If *n* is **null**, it simply returns **null**. If *n* has a left child, the method recurses on the left child; if there is no left child, *n* is returned.

```
 81
 82  // inorderSuccessor of node n in the BST
 83  //   is the leftmost child of the
 84  //   right child of n; returns null if n is
 85  //   null, OR no successor exists
 86  private BTnode inorderSuccessor(BTnode n){
 87      BTnode result = null;
 88      if (n != null) {
 89          if (n.right != null){
 90              result = Leftmost(n.right);
 91          }
 92      }
 93      return result;
 94  }
```

inorderSuccessor(BTnode n) is an example of a method calling a method. In a BST, if a successor exists, the in-order successor of any node is the leftmost descendant of its right child. Therefore, *n.right* is used as the argument to *Leftmost()*.

```
 96  // numberOfChildren returns:
 97  //    0 if both children of n null
 98  //    1 if one child is null
 99  //    2 if neither child null
100  private int numberOfChildren(BTnode n){
101      int result = 0;
102      if (n.left != null)
103          result++;
104      if (n.right != null) // both null
105          result++;
106      return result;
107  }
```

-250-

numberOfChildren(BTnode n) is a simple helper which keeps messy logic out of the main flow of *Delete()*. It simply counts the number of children attached to *n*, initializing its result to 0, then incrementing for each non-null child reference. Building small methods like this can be helpful in cleaning up already complex code by moving the implementation details into the separate method, rather than in the midst of the caller's complex logic.

```
109 //FindParent looks for a node with
110 // n as a child; root has no parent (return null)
111 private BTnode FindParent(BTnode n){
112    BTnode result = null;
113    if ((n != null) &&
114        (n != root)) {
115       result = FindParentR(root, n);
116    }
117    return result;
118 }
```

The *FindParent(BTnode n)* initializes the data needed for a call to the recursive *FindParentR()* helper method. It makes sure *n* is neither **null** nor the *root*, then returns the recursive method result.

FindParentR() does an exhaustive search through the BST, stopping either when a node is found which has *n* as either its left child or right child, or when all the nodes in the BST have been checked. Practically, the method should never fail, because the node *n* passed as a parameter is already known to be not **null**, and the node reference came from somewhere in the tree, so it must exist already as some other node's child (since it is already known that *n* is not the *root*).

```
120 //FindParentR is recursive helper
121 //for FindParent.  Does EXHAUSTIVE SEARCH for
122 //  p, where n is a child of p.  Assumes n exists
123 //   in the tree, and is not root
124 private BTnode FindParentR(BTnode p, BTnode n) {
125    BTnode result = null;
126    if (p != null) { //null p means stop
127       if ((p.left == n) ||  //n is a child of p
128           (p.right == n))
129          result = p;
130       else
131          // look for n down left
132          result = FindParentR(p.left,n);
133          // if not in left side
134          if (result == null)
135             // look for n on right
136             result = FindParentR(p.right,n);
137    }
138    return result;
139 }
```

FindParentR() checks parameter node *p* to see if parameter *n* is its child. A **null** *p* halts the search at this branch. If *n* is the right or left child (line 127-128) *p* is saved as the *result* of this method. If no match was found, the search continues recursively down *p.left*, and if that is unsuccessful, *p.right* is recursively searched as well.

Summary of BST Deletion Implementation

This concludes the discussion of the rather complex BST deletion process. Although each deletion potentially requires multiple searches for parent nodes, the entire process can be done in *O(n)* time, where *n* is the size of the tree. It could be made more efficient if parent references were included in every node, making the parent-finding process trivial and almost cost-free.

DELETION IN THE BST

In a relatively static BST, where the data is being inserted and deleted relatively infrequently compared to the number of times it is being searched, the computing cost of changing the tree are relatively negligible. However, in a relatively dynamic BST environment, where the tree is being continually modified when compared to the number of searches being done, further optimization of the modification process may be mandated. Marking deleted nodes as such, without actually re-structuring the tree until a more opportune time, when other processing such as searching, is not taking place, is one possibility. Adding a parent reference also improves performance by saving the extra reference in exchange for reduced search processing time.

Chapter Checklist

- ❏ BST Deletion can be complex because of the inter-relationships between the nodes, and the importance of maintaining the *BST Property* whenever a node is removed. There are three different cases to be considered when deleting a node, based on how many children it has.

- ❏ If the node to be deleted has **no children**, it may be deleted simply by setting the reference from its parent to **null.**

- ❏ If the node being deleted has **one child**, the deletion can be completed by replacing the deleted node, changing its parent's reference to instead reference its one child.

- ❏ Deleting a node having two children is more complicated. The node is replaced with its in-order successor node. The children of the deleted node become the children of the successor node, and the right child of the successor, if that child exists, becomes the left child of the successor's original parent.

- ❏ Designing a method can be facilitated by *abstracting* any helper methods it needs, simply defining their *interfaces* (behavior and return types) and treating them as if they had already been created. This defers the need to think about the helpers' implementation details, and allows the designer to focus on designing the method at hand without being distracted by the minutiae of figuring out how other methods will work.

> If debugging is the process of removing bugs, then programming must be the process of putting them in.
> – Edsger Dijkstra

Chapter 23: Heaps

The *Heap* data structure does not *sound* very structured, and the idea is more commonly associated with the standard office filing system employed by computer science instructors... heaps! But the *Heap* is a useful computer construct which allows data to be prioritized so that the most valuable item is always easy to find.

Strictly speaking, the *Heap* is *not* an ADT, but a particular kind of tree-based data structure with well-defined algorithms for inserting and removing nodes. An ADT typically omits such details as specifying particular algorithms for its methods.

The Heap Class Interface

The *Heap* interface is quite simple, requiring:

void insert(int n) - *Adds a new value, n, to the Heap.*

int remove() - *Removes the highest valued element from the Heap.*

and, for completeness:

int size() - *Returns the number of nodes contained in the Heap.*

boolean isEmpty() - *returns* ***true*** *if there are no values in the Heap.*

The Heap Property

A *Heap* is commonly implemented as a binary tree which exhibits the *Heap property*, which is: **at each node in the tree, each child has a lower value than its parent.** Although at first glance, this may sound a lot like the characteristics of a BST, the *Heap Property* is less restrictive than the *BST Property*, and allows the Heap's tree to be less tightly organized. Also, **every Heap is a *complete binary tree*, so that only the highest level can be missing any nodes, and only from the rightmost end.**

An example of a *Heap* is shown in Figure 76. The reader should confirm that (1) the *Heap Property* is maintained in this example, and (2) the Heap is a complete tree. Those familiar with the arrangement of nodes in a BST sometimes find the placement of larger values, such as '48', in the left half of the Heap somewhat disturbing. But recall that the *Heap Property* simply states that at any node, its descendants have lower values than that node. Inspection of the example will show that the property holds in this Figure. Also, note that the Heaps, generally, are not unique for a given set of data values, and may still retain their characteristics with a different arrangement of the same values. For example, in Figure 76, values '48' and '27' could be

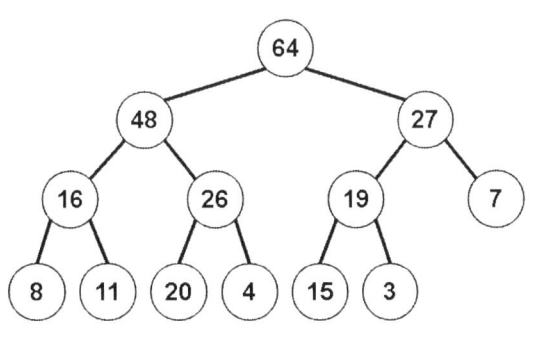

Figure 76: *Heap example*

exchanged, and the resulting tree would still be a Heap.

The creation of a Heap from a list of known data can be done by a human very easily through the following steps:

>   1) Sort the data in descending order;
>   2) Create a blank, complete binary tree containing as many nodes as there are values;
>   3) Place the sorted values into the blank tree from left to right, top to bottom order.

As an example, consider the set of values:

>   **12, 8, 23, 16, 33, 21, 5**

First, the data is sorted in descending order:

>   **33, 23, 21, 16, 12, 8, 5**

Next, an empty, complete binary tree is created. Conveniently, a seven node complete tree is also a full tree. Finally, the values are written into the tree from left to right, working downward level by level. The result is the Heap shown in Figure 77.

If all of the data to be placed into the heap is known ahead of time, it is easy to create the heap, as the largest value, which will be placed at the root, is already determined because the data has been sorted. More realistically, data will be added to and deleted from a Heap after it has been constructed, so it is important to learn the *insert()* and *remove()* algorithms so that they can be implemented in code.

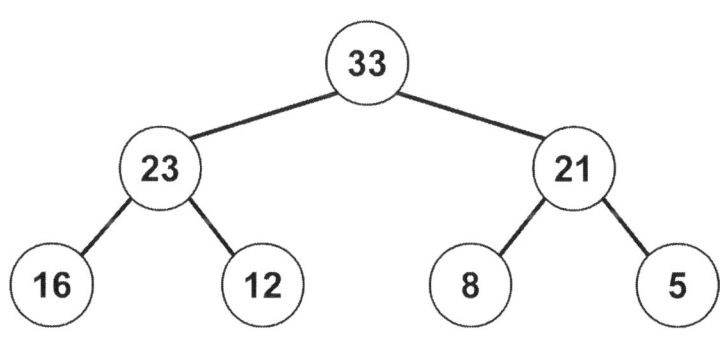

Figure 77: *Heap constructed using the algorithm discussed*

The Heap Insert Algorithm

Recalling that the Heap is always maintained as a complete tree, every node is added initially to the highest level of the tree in the next available slot which will ensure completeness of the tree. Next, the new node is 'trickled up' the tree, swapping its value with its parent value if it is larger than its parent. The value is followed to the former parent, and the check is made on the new parent (the grandparent, actually, of the originally added node). This continues until the value has risen as high as possible, potentially even becoming the new root value.

Figure 78 shows the process of adding the values 28 and 47 to the Heap pictured in Figure 77. The value 28 is added to keep the tree complete. 28 and 16 swap, moving 28 up. 28 is greater than 23, so it is again swapped, but because 33 is larger, the 28 remains where it is. When 47 is subsequently added, again keeping the tree complete, it is swapped with the 23, then is swapped with the 28, and finally reaches the root after swapping with 33.

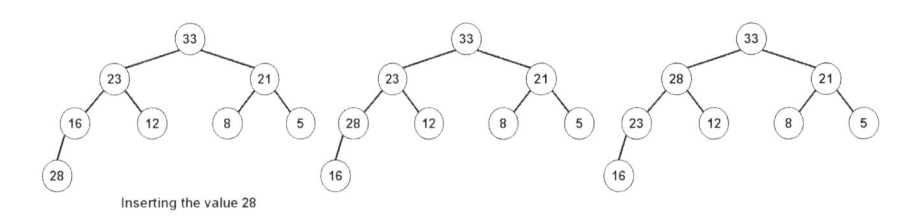

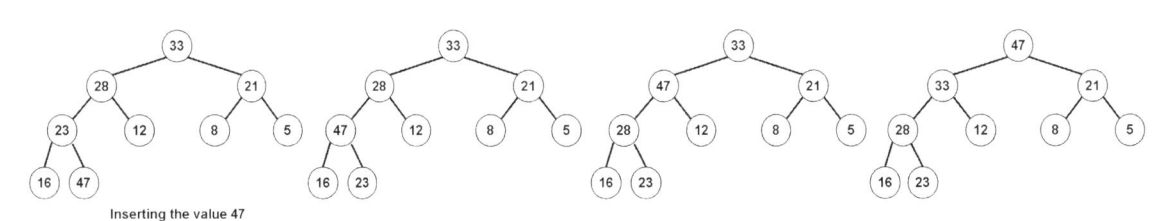

*Figure 78: Examples of adding **28** and **47** to the Heap of Figure 77*

The Heap Remove Algorithm

There is never any decision required when removing from the Heap, because **the root is always the node removed when removing from the Heap.** The process first saves the root value to be returned. Next, the value in the last-added node (the rightmost node on the highest level) is copied into the root node, and the node is removed. Next, the value at the root is 'trickled down' the tree. The root is compared to its larger child, and if the child is greater than the root, they swap values. This continues, following the value down through the tree until it is greater than both of its children, and stops moving.

Figure 79 shows two deletion operations on the Heap result shown in Figure 78. The first call to *Remove()* causes 47 to be returned, and the value from the rightmost bottom node, 23, becomes the root, as that node is removed from the tree. The larger of 23's children is 33, and because it is greater than 23, the values swap. 28 is 23's larger child, and is greater, so they are swapped, bringing 23 to its final level. The second *Remove()* call returns 33, and brings value 16 to the root, deleting its node from the tree. A swap occurs between 16 and 28, making 28 the new root. Because 16 is less than its child, 23, it swaps again, and ends up at the highest level (bottom) of the tree.

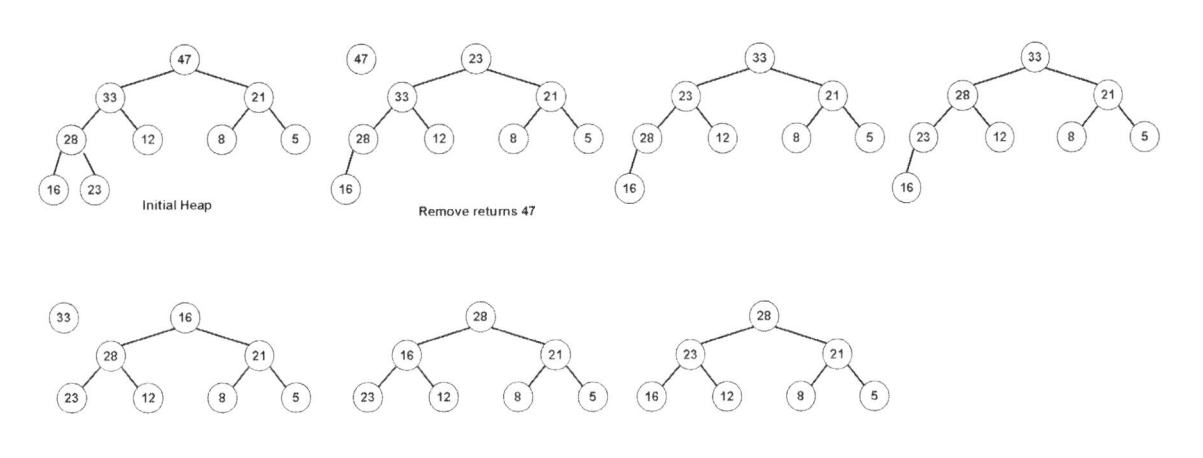

Figure 79: Result of two remove operations on final Heap from Figure 78

Implementing the Heap

It is evident from the *Insert()* and *Remove()* algorithm descriptions that the movement of the nodes requires repeated referencing of parent nodes. As such, implementing this structure as a linked tree is complicated and somewhat impractical. It also provides a great example of using an array structure to represent a tree!

It is possible to associate the tree node positions with the indices of an array containing the tree's values. First, the root is always located at the 0 index of the array. Suppose a node *n* is located at index *i*. **The array will be built so that the left child of *n* will always be located at index *2*i+1*, and the right child will be at index *2*i+2*.** Comparing the array to the Heap drawing, it is clear that 28, the root, is located at slot 0. Its left child, 23, is in slot *2*0+1 = 1*, and the left child, 21, is in slot *2*0+2 = 2*. The value 23 is in slot *1*, and its children, 16 and 12, are in slots *2*1+1 = 3* and *2*1+2 = 4*, respectively. This arrangement works for any binary tree, and **when the tree is a *complete* binary tree, there are no gaps in the array**. Another feature is that **the parent of the node at index *i* is located at *(i-1)/2*.** Because of the truncation done by Java when integers are divided, it is thus possible to calculate the index of any node's parent. The parent of node 5, located in slot 6 is *(6-1)/2 = 2*, and the parent of node 8, in slot 5, is *(5-1)/2 = 2* also, as these two nodes are siblings.

Index	Values
0	28
1	23
2	21
3	16
4	12
5	8
6	5

Figure 80: Array representation of the final Heap shown in Figure 79

Yet another advantage of this array implementation is that **when adding to keep the tree complete, the new node is simply added to the end of the list of used values.** As will be seen in the implementation for the Heap, this makes easy the things that would be difficult in a linked-node implementation of the Heap.

HEAPS

Implementing the Heap Using an Array

The code below implements an array-based Heap:

```
1
2  public class HeapA {
3     private int[] array; //int storage
4     private int last;    //index of last used slot
5     public HeapA(){
6         array = new int[100];
7         last = -1;        //empty indicator
8     }
```

The class fields are a private **int** array, appropriately name *array*, and an **int** counter, *last*, which holds the index of the last array slot in use. The constructor allocates the array to an arbitrary 100 slots, and *last* is set to -1 to indicate an empty Heap.

```
 9     //print level-order traversal
10     public void display(){
11         for (int i=0;i<=last;i++)
12             System.out.println(i+": "+array[i]);
13     }
```

The *display()* method included above simply prints out the array contents in sequence. This is an example of a forth type of tree traversal, the *level-order traversal*, which prints the nodes from left to right, top to bottom... exactly the order in which the array stores the values.

```
14     //return size of tree
15     public int size(){
16         return last+1;
17     }
```

The number of nodes in the tree is always one more than the value of *last*.

```
18      //true if tree has no nodes
19      public boolean isEmpty(){
20           return last < 0;
21      }
```

The *isEmpty()* method is simple to implement, based on the contents of *last*.

```
22      //add new value to heap
23      public void Insert(int value){
24           last++;
25           array[last] = value;
26           trickleUp(last);
27      }
```

Insert(int value) adds the new value to the end of the array, first incrementing *last*, then putting the new value into *array[last]*. Then, it calls *trickleUp(last)*, which recursively moves the value at *last* up through its branch until its parent's value is larger than its own. *TrickleUp()* is shown below.

```
28      //remove root value from heap
29      public int Remove(){
30           int result = array[0];
31           array[0] = array[last];
32           last--;
33           trickleDown(0);
34           return result;
35      }
```

Equally simple is the *Remove()* method. It saves as its *result* the root value in slot 0. Then, because the last node added is always located at *array[last]*, it moves that value to the root (line 31), and decrements *last* to delete the last node (line 32). It then calls *trickleDown(0)*, which allows the new root value to sink until its value is larger than either of its children.

Three simple methods were written to make it easy to obtain the index of a node's parent or either child.

```
36    //return the parent of index i
37    // -1 if parent of 0 attempted
38    private int parent(int i){
39        int result = -1;
40        if (i > 0)
41            result = (i -1) / 2;
42        return result;
43    }
```

parent(i) returns the index of the parent of slot *i*. If *i* is the root, it returns -1 to indicate there is no parent.

```
44    //left child index of index i
45    private int leftchild(int i){
46        return  2*i +1;
47    }
48    //right child index of index i
49    private int rightchild(int i){
50        return  2*i +2;
51    }
```

leftchild(i) and *rightchild(i)* return the index of the left or right child of slot *i*. In practical usage, the caller of either method should verify that the value returned does not exceed the allocated size of the array before using it to access the array.

```
52      // starting at index i, swap with
53      // parent if array[i] > array[parent(i)]
54      private void trickleUp(int i){
55          int temp; //hold for swap
56          if (i > 0){ //cannot trickle up from root
57              if (array[i] > array[parent(i)]){//do swap
58                  temp = array[i];
59                  array[i] = array[parent(i)];
60                  array[parent(i)] = temp;
61                  //recursive call to continue
62                  trickleUp(parent(i));
63              }
64          }
65      }
```

trickleUp(i) is simple due to its use of recursion. Its purpose, as described earlier, is to move the value at slot *i* upward through the tree until it is located such that its parent node has a greater value than its own. The *temp* variable is used for swapping the node and its parent if necessary. The method and any further recursion halts when parameter *i* reaches 0, the root of the tree (line 56). It is important to note that the recursive call at line 62 is inside of the **if** statement comparing the slot at *i* with the slot at *parent(i)* (line 57). If *array[i]* is larger than its parent, the values are swapped, and *trickleUp()* continues recursively, now checking the parent slot with its parent, and so on until either the child is smaller than the parent, or the value has risen all the way to the root.

HEAPS

```
66  //starting at i, swap array[i]
67  //with its largest child, if child
68  //is greater
69  private void trickleDown(int i){
70     int swap, temp;
71     int left = leftchild(i);
72     int right = rightchild(i);
73     if (right > last) //right may not exist
74        right = left;
75     //keep from going off end
76     if (i <= parent(last)){
77        //find index of larger child
78        if (array[left] > array[right])
79           swap = left;
80        else
81           swap = right;
82        //swap is index of larger child
83        if (array[swap]> array[i]){ //child larger, do swap
84           temp = array[swap];
85           array[swap] = array[i];
86           array[i]= temp;
87           //recursive call to continue
88           trickleDown(swap);
89        }
90     }
91  }
92  } //end of HeapA class
```

trickleDown(i) moves the value at slot *i* down through the tree by exchanging it with its larger child, if that child is greater than the node itself. First, in lines 71-72, the results of method calls to *leftchild()* and *rightchild()* are stored in *left* and *right*, respectively. This illustrates an efficiency consideration which some programmers may overlook: calling a method takes considerably more processing time than accessing a variable by name. By calling the methods once (lines 71-72) and saving the results, the variables can be used, rather than repeating the calls, in lines 78, 79, and 81[d]. Lines 73-74 prevent an error which could occur if node *i* happens to be in the next-to-last level of the tree, and has no right child. The check at line 76 ensures that the recursion will stop by preventing the processing of *i* if its children would fall outside of the active range of the array stored in *last*. But if *last* indexes a left child, the *parent(last)* could try access a right child, which contains unreliable, deleted data. In lines 77-81, the index *swap* is set to the index of the larger of slot *i*'s two children. If slot *swap* is greater than the value at slot *i*, the values are exchanged and, as done in *trickleUp()*, a recursive call is made on the child index indicated by *swap* to trickle if further down if necessary (lines 83-88).

Variations: the Max-Heap and the Min-Heap

In the preceding *Heap* discussions, the root of the node was said to always contain the largest value in the *Heap*. This is the most common kind of Heap implemented, and it is more specifically referred to as a *Max-Heap*, because the maximum value in the data set is always placed at the root. Similarly, the *Heap Property* is more accurately called the *Max-Heap Property*, for the same reason.

It is also possible to analogously create a *Min-Heap* in which the minimum value is always placed at the root and thus removed at the next *Remove()* operation. The *Min-Heap Property* states: **at each node in the tree, each child has a greater value than its parent.** Implementing the *Min-Heap* involves exactly the same algorithms as presented for the *Heap*, except that *trickleUp()* must check to see that the parent node is always less than the current node to determine whether to swap, and *trickleDown()* must select the lower-valued child node for swapping if it is less than the current node. Figure 81 shows a Min-Heap built from the same data as in the Max-Heap, Figure 77.

---

[d] Although saving a few method calls may seem like an insignificant speed consideration in this particular example, in high-performance applications every reduction in execution speed can be essential. Recognizing such efficiency issues as code is being written is a characteristic of good programming practice.

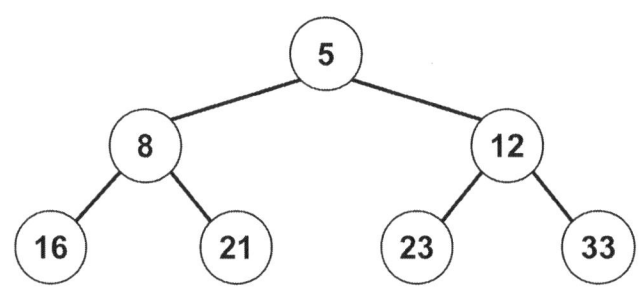

Figure 81: Min-Heap constructed from data in Figure 77 Max-Heap

Applications of the Heap

Two examples of using the Heap are sorting values and implementing a *priority queue*. In the case of sorting, the *Big-O* performance when using a heap is at the theoretical minimum— as good as can be obtained. For the *priority queue*, described below, the Heap provides a fast, efficient storage mechanism.

Sorting With the Heap

When considering *Heap* performance, insertion is $O(log_2(n))$ because the number of comparisons required by any newly added node in the trickle-up is related to the height of the tree, not the total number of nodes in the tree. Removal from a *Heap* is also $O(log_2(n))$ for the same reason, applied to the trickle-down. This heap sort consists of adding all the data elements to the heap, which requires an insertion for each of the *n* elements, which is $O(nlog_2(n))$. Then each of the *n* elements is removed, which returns them in sorted order, another $O(nlog_2(n))$ process. However, $O(nlog_2(n))$ is simply, in this notation, the same as $O(nlog_2(n))$, the theoretical minimum time complexity for any general sorting algorithm. (Notice that this is an improvement over the earlier $O(n^2)$ complexity for the selection- and bubble- sorts.)

Implementing a *Priority Queue ADT* Using the Heap

A variant of the *Queue* ADT discussed previously is the *Priority Queue (P-Queue)* ADT. While the standard *Queue* is a Last-In, First-Out (LIFO) structure, the *P- Queue* might be described as a Last-In, Best-Out structure. Conceptually, the *P-Queue* has the same interfaced methods as a *Queue*, *size()*, *isEmpty()*, *insert()* and *remove()*, but the behavior of *remove()* is such that, instead of the first-added item being removed, the item with highest priority of all those in the queue is the one that is returned. An example of this in real-life would be an organized person's daily task list, where, ideally, the most important item on the list is the one done next, rather than the less-important ones which were added earliest. Another example might be a multi-tasking computer operating system (such as Windows), which has a job list of the multiple programs it is running at the 'same time', and devotes some processing time to each of the programs in succession, with the highest-priority jobs always selected before the lower-priority ones[e].

One of the problems with a *P-Queue* is that, if high-priority items are continually being added, the already-existing low priority items will *never* be selected for removal. For this reason, in practical applications the node evaluation function may involve a more sophisticated algorithm related to both a priority value and an 'age' measure. In this scheme, items which have been in the *P-Queue* for longer than a certain length of time will be given a higher value, even though their priority is low, which moves them up in the queue so that they will, eventually, be removed. The major functions of the *P-Queue* remain the same.

On the surface, it may seem that a *Heap* **is** a *P-Queue* already, but this is not so. The *P-Queue* ADT does not specify how it is to be implemented. It would be quite reasonable, for example, to modify the implementation of a standard linked queue implementation so that, on a remove operation, the entire list is searched for the largest value, and then *that* value is removed, rather than the front item. However, using the *Heap* allows a much more efficient, simple implementation.

The code to implement a *P-Queue* given an existing *Heap* class is simple, basically wrapping a new interface around the *Heap*:

---

[e] Often, an operating system does not strictly use a *P-Queue*, but rather, a customized variant, in order to ensure that all jobs get some processing, even low-priority ones.

HEAPS

```
Class PQueue {
   private Heap sotrage;
   //constructor
   PQueue() {
      storage = new Heap();
   }
```

The constructor initializes the underlying *Heap* used for storing the queue data.

```
   //add to queue
   public void insert(int x){
      storage.insert(x);
   }
   //remove best value from queue
   public int remove(){
      return storage.remove(x);
   }
   //is it empty?
   public boolean is Empty(){
      return storage.isEmpty(x);
   }
   //size of queue
   public int size(){
      return storage.size();
   }
```

All of the *P-Queue* methods are simply wrapper calls to the corresponding *Heap* methods which do the actual work. The purpose here is to again illustrate the ability to create an interface as a wrapper, even, as in this case, just an appropriate class name, *PQueue*, around an existing class in order to implement an ADT.

Chapter Checklist

- ❏ A *Heap* is a tree-based data structure (not an ADT) which specifies the interfaced methods: *insert()*, *remove()*, *isempty()*, and *size()*. The tree exhibits two essential properties: 1) the *Heap Property* says that **at each node in the tree, each child has a lower value than its parent**, and 2) **every Heap is a complete binary tree**

- ❏ An algorithm to create a *Heap* from a set of known data is: 1) Sort the data in descending order; 2) Create a blank, complete binary tree containing as many nodes as there are values; 3) Place the sorted values into the blank tree from left to right, top to bottom order.

- ❏ The algorithm to insert a single data item into a *Heap* is: 1) add a new node with the new value to the highest tree level, maintaining a *complete* tree, 2) allow the new value to 'trickle-up' the tree until its parent's value is larger than its value, or it has become the root.

- ❏ The algorithm to remove a single data item from a *Heap* is: 1) Save the root value to be returned, 2) Remove the bottom, rightmost node, and put its value into the root, 3) Starting at the root, let the value trickle down through its larger child node until its value is greater than the value of either of its children.

- ❏ A *complete* tree can easily be stored in an array with no gaps, where, for node *i*, the left child of n will always be located at index *2*i+1*, and the right child will be at index *2*i+2*. The parent of *i* is located at *(i-1)/2*.

- ❏ Sorting can be done efficiently in **$O(nlog_2(n))$** by placing the data into the *Heap*, then removing it in sorted order.

- ❏ A *Priority Queue* is easily implemented as a wrapper class around a *Heap*.

> **He who loves practice without theory is like the sailor who boards ship without a rudder and compass and never knows where he may cast.**
> *– Leonardo da Vinci*

Chapter 24: Conclusion

Outstanding software engineers are those who have invested the time to acquire understanding beyond the low-level syntax of a programming language and the ability to simply *write a program*. In addition, they understand the 'big picture' of what distinguishes a good program from a bad one, and can use criteria for measuring quality, such as those defined by the **FEMUR** mnemonic. They know what problem solving is, and how to apply a methodology like the **Requirements, Design, Implement, Test** sequence to create a quality problem solution.

Experts in software development use **abstraction** and **Abstract Data Types** because these aid design and development by postponing the consideration of details, and instead focus on higher-level, conceptual functionality. They have learned the standard, conventional types such as the **Double-ended List**, **Stack**, **Queue**, **Binary Search Tree**, and **Heap**, and use them as design elements, either directly or in custom variations, as necessary. They also know the algorithms for the basic operations within each standard ADT, and can implement them by deriving the code from their understanding of what they are trying to accomplish.

The best programmers recognize **data structures** as building-blocks for the implementation of their design. They are familiar with the **native types** of their chosen language, and can construct aggregate data types using (in Java) the **class** and **object** elements. They can distinguish between **classes**, **objects**, and **object references**, and are comfortable using them. Array structures are simple for them to use, because they understand indexed structures, and how to move and sort the data in them. Linked-structures do not intimidate them, and they are comfortable with objects referencing each other. They can analyze algorithms for time complexity and efficiency, and make informed decisions about the most effective approach to use in coding the algorithm.

It is hoped that *Designing Data Structures in Java* has been an effective resource in providing the starting point for the beginning student to advance toward a mastery of the fundamentals of program development. Such proficiency develops over time, and only with consistent, persistent effort on the part of the learner. May you be inspired toward excellence in your pursuit of programming and engineering software.

INDEX

Abstract Data Type 57, 61
Abstraction 23, 27, 29, 57
Acyclic 210, 214
ADT 41, 57-61, 63-66, 74, 75, 85, 89, 91, 115, 117, 118, 121, 123, 125, 127, 128, 133,
            135, 140, 143-145, 148, 149, 160, 162-165, 176, 177, 185, 186, 255, 267-270
Algorithm 24, 25, 91, 92, 95-97, 100, 101, 103, 104, 106, 107, 110, 111, 219, 222-224,
                                                    230, 249, 257-260, 267, 268, 270
Allocation 43, 141, 152, 185
Array . . 41-56, 63, 68-72, 74, 75, 81, 83, 84, 87, 89, 91-93, 95-97, 100, 104, 109-113, 118-
            122, 128-130, 133, 134, 141-143, 177, 180, 196, 197, 260-263, 266, 270
ArrayUtils 44, 45, 51, 72, 73, 85, 88
Big-O 104-107, 110, 267
Big-O notation 104, 106, 107
Binary Search 110, 111, 113, 141, 215, 217, 218, 222, 223, 226, 230
Binary Search Tree 215, 217, 218, 222, 230
Binary Search Tree Property 215, 218, 222
Binary searches 109
Binary tree 209-216, 225, 228-232, 234, 235, 256, 257, 260, 270
BST 215-230, 234, 235, 237, 241-244, 248-254, 256
BST Property 224, 227, 229, 230, 242, 254, 256
Bubble sort 96-101, 104
Chess 25, 26
Classes 11, 21, 33, 35, 39, 40, 59-61, 105, 148, 160, 163, 164
Coding 18, 57, 60, 198, 248
Cohesion 20-22
Common error 36
Complete binary tree 228-230, 256, 257, 260, 270
Complexity 17, 104, 106, 107, 110, 113, 241, 242, 267
Connected 149, 209-212, 214, 241, 242
Data Abstraction 27, 57

-273-

Data hiding	44, 59, 61, 217
Data Structures	1, 11, 12, 17, 31, 41, 57, 209, 214
Data Type	32, 33, 39, 41, 43, 57, 61, 65, 115, 175, 248
Decoupling	20-22
Degree	17, 19, 103, 163, 209, 210, 214, 215
Design	15-18, 20, 22, 58, 63, 75, 103, 131, 163, 164, 248, 249
Details	14, 16, 22, 23, 27, 28, 39, 57, 58, 61, 63, 76, 118, 123, 127, 135, 145, 148, 163, 233, 244, 248, 249, 251, 254, 255
Directed Graph	210
Divide and conquer	189, 195, 198
Double ended list	143, 161
Doubly-linked	199-203, 208, 216
Droste effect	188
Dynamic linked list	137, 143, 175, 177
Efficiency	17, 19, 21, 22, 104, 107, 109, 161, 199, 265, 266
Encapsulation	20, 59
Evaluating algorithms	103
Exhaustive search	237, 240, 251, 252
Factorial	105, 191-193, 198
FEMUR	19-22
FIFO	125, 135, 161
First-in, First-out	135
Full binary tree	229, 230
Functionality	17-22, 33, 115, 229
Good programming	12, 46, 266
Graph	209, 210, 214
Heap	255-262, 266-270, 272
Heap Property	256, 266, 270
Heap sort	267
Height of a tree	211, 235

INDEX

Helper methods 243, 249, 254
Implement 11, 15, 22, 56, 57, 59-61, 75, 140, 162-164, 215, 223, 262, 268, 269
IndexedList 63-66, 68-71, 74, 75
Interface . . . 18, 21, 41, 57-59, 61, 63, 64, 66, 68, 74-77, 85, 115, 118, 121, 123, 125, 127, 135, 143-145, 148, 160-164, 166, 170, 177, 186, 194, 217, 235, 237, 238, 255, 268, 269
In-degree 210
In-order successor 242-244, 246, 249, 250, 254
In-order Traversal 233-235, 240, 242
Last-in, First-out 123, 267
LIFO 115, 123, 160, 267
Linear search 109, 110, 113
Linked list . . 137, 139-143, 145, 148, 149, 151, 165, 175-177, 180, 186, 194, 195, 198-203, 208, 216
LinkedList 144, 145, 149, 150, 159-162
Looking for stuff 16, 18, 19, 22, 104, 106
Maintainability 19, 21
Max-Heap 266, 267
Memory 19, 21, 32-35, 37, 38, 40, 41, 56, 91, 103, 137, 138, 141, 142, 173, 180, 193, 213, 214
Min-Heap 266, 267
Murphy's law 59
Node . . . 137-140, 142, 149-155, 157-160, 165-171, 173-176, 178-186, 194, 195, 199-201, 204-208, 210-212, 214-219, 221-238, 240-247, 249-252, 254, 256-260, 262, 264-268, 270
Object 27, 28, 31, 33-42, 51, 60, 138, 139, 142, 147, 152, 160, 176, 199, 200
Object References 34-36, 41
Objects 11, 17, 31, 33, 35, 37, 38, 40-42, 56, 60, 137, 149, 180
OOP 60, 61
Ordered list 75-77, 126, 177, 185

OrderedList 75-77, 79, 81, 82, 89, 91, 177, 178, 180, 181, 183, 185, 186
Out-degree 210
Post-order Traversal 234, 240
Pre-order Traversal 231-233, 236-238, 240
Priority Queue 267, 270
Problem representation 24
Problem solving 13, 14, 22, 23, 57, 60, 189, 248
Program design 17, 22, 248
Program implementation 18, 22
Program testing 22
Quality 14, 19, 20, 22
Queue 121, 125-135, 160-162, 165, 170-176, 267-270
Recursion 187-191, 193-196, 198, 216-219, 228, 232-235, 238, 264, 266
Recursive algorithms 210, 213, 214, 216
Reference variable 34-36, 38-40, 42, 138, 139, 142, 153, 176, 183, 186
Reliability 17, 19, 21, 22, 59
Representation 15, 23-27, 29, 34, 139, 260
Requirements 16-20, 22, 103, 107, 222
Requirements Analysis 16, 18, 22
Reverse method 118
Roman numerals 24-26
Selection sort 91-95, 97, 100, 101, 104, 195, 196
Singly-linked 199-201, 208
Software Development Process 14-16
Software engineering 1, 12, 14, 15, 20, 22, 162
Sorting 75, 91, 96, 101, 104, 198, 215, 267, 270
Stack . . . 41, 115-123, 125, 127, 128, 130, 133, 160-162, 165-170, 175, 176, 191, 193, 198
Summation 46, 47, 52
Testing 16, 18, 19, 22, 164
Time complexity 104, 106, 107, 110, 113, 267

INDEX

Traversal 142, 198, 208, 212, 214, 231-238, 240, 242, 261
Tree traversal 231, 261
UnorderedList 75, 76, 80, 81, 89
Usability 17, 19, 21, 22
Visual recursion 188
Waterfall 15
Wrapper class 162-164, 270

DESIGNING DATA STRUCTURES IN JAVA